Mental Health Daily Journal

365 Pages for a Year of Journaling

Designed by

Abbie Brasch

Introduction

This journal is designed to help track the state of your mental health each day through noting medication changes and by journaling about any fluctuating feelings and habits. Acknowledging the good days and the not-so-good days helps support our mental health journey. By keeping track of the changes in our lives, we are better able to understand our patterns and how shifts in our external and internal world can affect our mental health for better or for worse.

With this new edition of Mental Health Daily Journal, you are now able to also write about your monthly goals or reflect on each month as it passes.

Using this journal can also assist the health care professionals aiding you on your journey. With details on how medication, supplements, activities and daily circumstances are serving your mental health, health care professionals can better understand your inner world as you navigate your mental health journey one day at a time and therefore be able to treat you accordingly.

Although using this journal daily is ideal, it is not intended to be an added pressure in your life. Those of us suffering from mental health difficulties tend to be extremely hard on ourselves so this journal is not about trying to be perfect. It is about acknowledging where you are today no matter how you are feeling. This journal should be a place where you can bring your whole self and express as much or as little as you want to without apology.

You can write in this journal every day, once a month, once a year, or whenever you feel like it. It is here to aid and support you on your healing journey in a way that works for you.

I hope it serves you well.

Medication Strattera 20mg , Lexapro 10mg   Adjustments -5 mg Lexapro

Supplements multivitamin, fish oil, vitamin b12

Self-Care This can be anything from exercising to meditating to taking a nap

Best Thing That Happened Today _____

Day of Cycle ___23___   Moon Phase Waning Pisces

How I'm Feeling 1 2 3 4 5 6 7 8 9 10

Write as much or as little as you would like about your day
and how you are feeling.

January

February

March

April

May

June

July

August

September

October

November

December

Date _____

Medication _____   Adjustments _____

_____

Supplements _____

_____

Self-Care _____

_____

Best Thing That Happened Today _____

_____

Day of Cycle _____   Moon Phase _____

How I'm Feeling 1 2 3 4 5 6 7 8 9 10

_____

_____

_____

_____

_____

_____

_____

_____

_____

_____

_____

_____

_____

_____

_____

_____

_____

_____

_____

_____

_____

_____

Date _____

Medication _____   Adjustments _____

_____

Supplements _____

_____

Self-Care _____

_____

Best Thing That Happened Today _____

_____

Day of Cycle _____   Moon Phase _____

How I'm Feeling 1 2 3 4 5 6 7 8 9 10

_____

_____

_____

_____

_____

_____

_____

_____

_____

_____

_____

_____

_____

_____

_____

_____

_____

_____

_____

_____

_____

_____

_____

Date _____

Medication _____   Adjustments _____

_____

Supplements _____

_____

Self-Care _____

_____

Best Thing That Happened Today _____

_____

Day of Cycle _____   Moon Phase _____

How I'm Feeling 1 2 3 4 5 6 7 8 9 10

_____
_____
_____
_____
_____
_____
_____
_____
_____
_____
_____
_____
_____
_____
_____
_____
_____
_____
_____
_____
_____
_____
_____
_____
_____

Date _____

Medication _____   Adjustments _____

_____

Supplements _____

_____

Self-Care _____

_____

Best Thing That Happened Today _____

_____

Day of Cycle _____   Moon Phase _____

How I'm Feeling 1 2 3 4 5 6 7 8 9 10

_____

_____

_____

_____

_____

_____

_____

_____

_____

_____

_____

_____

_____

_____

_____

_____

_____

_____

_____

_____

_____

_____

_____

Date _____

Medication _____   Adjustments _____

_____

Supplements _____

_____

Self-Care _____

_____

Best Thing That Happened Today _____

_____

Day of Cycle _____   Moon Phase _____

How I'm Feeling 1 2 3 4 5 6 7 8 9 10

_____

_____

_____

_____

_____

_____

_____

_____

_____

_____

_____

_____

_____

_____

_____

_____

_____

_____

_____

_____

_____

_____

_____

Date _____

Medication _____   Adjustments _____

_____

Supplements _____

_____

Self-Care _____

_____

Best Thing That Happened Today _____

_____

Day of Cycle _____   Moon Phase _____

How I'm Feeling 1 2 3 4 5 6 7 8 9 10

_____

_____

_____

_____

_____

_____

_____

_____

_____

_____

_____

_____

_____

_____

_____

_____

_____

_____

_____

_____

_____

_____

_____

_____

_____

Date _____

Medication _____   Adjustments _____

_____

Supplements _____

_____

Self-Care _____

_____

Best Thing That Happened Today _____

_____

Day of Cycle _____   Moon Phase _____

How I'm Feeling 1 2 3 4 5 6 7 8 9 10

_____

_____

_____

_____

_____

_____

_____

_____

_____

_____

_____

_____

_____

_____

_____

_____

_____

_____

_____

_____

_____

_____

Date _____

Medication _____ Adjustments _____

_____

Supplements _____

_____

Self-Care _____

_____

Best Thing That Happened Today _____

_____

Day of Cycle _____ Moon Phase _____

How I'm Feeling 1 2 3 4 5 6 7 8 9 10

_____

_____

_____

_____

_____

_____

_____

_____

_____

_____

_____

_____

_____

_____

_____

_____

_____

_____

_____

_____

_____

_____

_____

Date _____

Medication_____ Adjustments _____

_____

Supplements _____

_____

Self-Care _____

_____

Best Thing That Happened Today _____

_____

Day of Cycle _____ Moon Phase_____

How I'm Feeling 1 2 3 4 5 6 7 8 9 10

_____

_____

_____

_____

_____

_____

_____

_____

_____

_____

_____

_____

_____

_____

_____

_____

_____

_____

_____

_____

_____

_____

Date _____

Medication _____   Adjustments _____

_____

Supplements _____

_____

Self-Care _____

_____

Best Thing That Happened Today _____

_____

Day of Cycle _____   Moon Phase _____

How I'm Feeling 1 2 3 4 5 6 7 8 9 10

_____

_____

_____

_____

_____

_____

_____

_____

_____

_____

_____

_____

_____

_____

_____

_____

_____

_____

_____

_____

_____

_____

Date _____

Medication _____   Adjustments _____

_____

Supplements _____

_____

Self-Care _____

_____

Best Thing That Happened Today _____

_____

Day of Cycle _____   Moon Phase _____

How I'm Feeling 1 2 3 4 5 6 7 8 9 10

_____
_____
_____
_____
_____
_____
_____
_____
_____
_____
_____
_____
_____
_____
_____
_____
_____
_____
_____
_____
_____
_____
_____

Date _____

Medication _____   Adjustments _____

_____

Supplements _____

_____

Self-Care _____

_____

Best Thing That Happened Today _____

_____

Day of Cycle _____   Moon Phase _____

How I'm Feeling 1 2 3 4 5 6 7 8 9 10

_____

_____

_____

_____

_____

_____

_____

_____

_____

_____

_____

_____

_____

_____

_____

_____

_____

_____

_____

_____

_____

_____

_____

_____

_____

Date _____

Medication_____   Adjustments _____

_____

Supplements _____

_____

Self-Care _____

_____

Best Thing That Happened Today _____

_____

Day of Cycle _____   Moon Phase_____

How I'm Feeling 1 2 3 4 5 6 7 8 9 10

_____

_____

_____

_____

_____

_____

_____

_____

_____

_____

_____

_____

_____

_____

_____

_____

_____

_____

_____

_____

_____

_____

_____

Date _____

Medication _____   Adjustments _____

_____

Supplements _____

_____

Self-Care _____

_____

Best Thing That Happened Today _____

_____

Day of Cycle _____   Moon Phase_____

How I'm Feeling 1 2 3 4 5 6 7 8 9 10

_____

_____

_____

_____

_____

_____

_____

_____

_____

_____

_____

_____

_____

_____

_____

_____

_____

_____

_____

_____

_____

_____

_____

Date _____

Medication _____   Adjustments _____

_____

Supplements _____

_____

Self-Care _____

_____

Best Thing That Happened Today _____

_____

Day of Cycle _____   Moon Phase _____

How I'm Feeling 1 2 3 4 5 6 7 8 9 10

_____

_____

_____

_____

_____

_____

_____

_____

_____

_____

_____

_____

_____

_____

_____

_____

_____

_____

_____

_____

_____

_____

_____

_____

Date _____

Medication _____   Adjustments _____

_____

Supplements _____

_____

Self-Care _____

_____

Best Thing That Happened Today _____

_____

Day of Cycle _____   Moon Phase_____

How I'm Feeling 1 2 3 4 5 6 7 8 9 10

_____

_____

_____

_____

_____

_____

_____

_____

_____

_____

_____

_____

_____

_____

_____

_____

_____

_____

_____

_____

_____

_____

_____

_____

Date _____

Medication _____   Adjustments _____

_____

Supplements _____

_____

Self-Care _____

_____

Best Thing That Happened Today _____

_____

Day of Cycle _____   Moon Phase_____

How I'm Feeling 1 2 3 4 5 6 7 8 9 10

_____

_____

_____

_____

_____

_____

_____

_____

_____

_____

_____

_____

_____

_____

_____

_____

_____

_____

_____

_____

_____

_____

_____

_____

Date _____

Medication _____   Adjustments _____
_____

Supplements _____
_____

Self-Care _____
_____

Best Thing That Happened Today _____
_____

Day of Cycle _____   Moon Phase_____

How I'm Feeling 1 2 3 4 5 6 7 8 9 10

_____
_____
_____
_____
_____
_____
_____
_____
_____
_____
_____
_____
_____
_____
_____
_____
_____
_____
_____
_____
_____
_____
_____
_____

Date _____

Medication _____   Adjustments _____

_____

Supplements _____

_____

Self-Care _____

_____

Best Thing That Happened Today _____

_____

Day of Cycle _____   Moon Phase _____

How I'm Feeling 1 2 3 4 5 6 7 8 9 10

_____

_____

_____

_____

_____

_____

_____

_____

_____

_____

_____

_____

_____

_____

_____

_____

_____

_____

_____

_____

_____

_____

_____

_____

Date _____

Medication _____ Adjustments _____

_____

Supplements _____

_____

Self-Care _____

_____

Best Thing That Happened Today _____

_____

Day of Cycle _____ Moon Phase _____

How I'm Feeling 1 2 3 4 5 6 7 8 9 10

_____
_____
_____
_____
_____
_____
_____
_____
_____
_____
_____
_____
_____
_____
_____
_____
_____
_____
_____
_____
_____
_____
_____
_____

Date _____

Medication _____   Adjustments _____

_____

Supplements _____

_____

Self-Care _____

_____

Best Thing That Happened Today _____

_____

Day of Cycle _____   Moon Phase _____

How I'm Feeling 1 2 3 4 5 6 7 8 9 10

_____

_____

_____

_____

_____

_____

_____

_____

_____

_____

_____

_____

_____

_____

_____

_____

_____

_____

_____

_____

_____

_____

_____

_____

_____

_____

Date _____

Medication _____   Adjustments _____

_____

Supplements _____

_____

Self-Care _____

_____

Best Thing That Happened Today _____

_____

Day of Cycle _____   Moon Phase _____

How I'm Feeling 1 2 3 4 5 6 7 8 9 10

_____

_____

_____

_____

_____

_____

_____

_____

_____

_____

_____

_____

_____

_____

_____

_____

_____

_____

_____

_____

_____

_____

_____

_____

_____

Date _____

Medication_____   Adjustments _____

_____

Supplements _____

_____

Self-Care _____

_____

Best Thing That Happened Today _____

_____

Day of Cycle _____   Moon Phase_____

How I'm Feeling 1 2 3 4 5 6 7 8 9 10

_____

_____

_____

_____

_____

_____

_____

_____

_____

_____

_____

_____

_____

_____

_____

_____

_____

_____

_____

_____

_____

_____

_____

_____

_____

_____

Date _____

Medication _____ Adjustments _____

_____

Supplements _____

_____

Self-Care _____

_____

Best Thing That Happened Today _____

_____

Day of Cycle _____ Moon Phase _____

How I'm Feeling 1 2 3 4 5 6 7 8 9 10

_____

_____

_____

_____

_____

_____

_____

_____

_____

_____

_____

_____

_____

_____

_____

_____

_____

_____

_____

_____

_____

_____

_____

Date _____

Medication _____   Adjustments _____

_____

Supplements _____

_____

Self-Care _____

_____

Best Thing That Happened Today _____

_____

Day of Cycle _____   Moon Phase _____

How I'm Feeling 1 2 3 4 5 6 7 8 9 10

_____

_____

_____

_____

_____

_____

_____

_____

_____

_____

_____

_____

_____

_____

_____

_____

_____

_____

_____

_____

_____

_____

_____

_____

Date _____

Medication _____   Adjustments _____

_____

Supplements _____

_____

Self-Care _____

_____

Best Thing That Happened Today _____

_____

Day of Cycle _____   Moon Phase _____

How I'm Feeling 1 2 3 4 5 6 7 8 9 10

_____

_____

_____

_____

_____

_____

_____

_____

_____

_____

_____

_____

_____

_____

_____

_____

_____

_____

_____

_____

_____

_____

_____

_____

Date _____

Medication _____   Adjustments _____

_____

Supplements _____

_____

Self-Care _____

_____

Best Thing That Happened Today _____

_____

Day of Cycle _____   Moon Phase _____

How I'm Feeling 1 2 3 4 5 6 7 8 9 10

_____

_____

_____

_____

_____

_____

_____

_____

_____

_____

_____

_____

_____

_____

_____

_____

_____

_____

_____

_____

_____

_____

_____

_____

Date _____

Medication _____   Adjustments _____
_____

Supplements _____
_____

Self-Care _____
_____

Best Thing That Happened Today _____
_____

Day of Cycle _____   Moon Phase_____

How I'm Feeling 1 2 3 4 5 6 7 8 9 10

_____
_____
_____
_____
_____
_____
_____
_____
_____
_____
_____
_____
_____
_____
_____
_____
_____
_____
_____
_____
_____
_____
_____
_____

Date _____

Medication _____   Adjustments _____

_____

Supplements _____

_____

Self-Care _____

_____

Best Thing That Happened Today _____

_____

Day of Cycle _____   Moon Phase _____

How I'm Feeling 1 2 3 4 5 6 7 8 9 10

_____
_____
_____
_____
_____
_____
_____
_____
_____
_____
_____
_____
_____
_____
_____
_____
_____
_____
_____
_____
_____
_____
_____
_____
_____
_____
_____

Date _____

Medication _____   Adjustments _____

_____

Supplements _____

_____

Self-Care _____

_____

Best Thing That Happened Today _____

_____

Day of Cycle _____   Moon Phase _____

How I'm Feeling 1 2 3 4 5 6 7 8 9 10

_____

_____

_____

_____

_____

_____

_____

_____

_____

_____

_____

_____

_____

_____

_____

_____

_____

_____

_____

_____

_____

_____

_____

_____

_____

Date _____

Medication _____   Adjustments _____

_____

Supplements _____

_____

Self-Care _____

_____

Best Thing That Happened Today _____

_____

Day of Cycle _____   Moon Phase_____

How I'm Feeling 1 2 3 4 5 6 7 8 9 10

_____

_____

_____

_____

_____

_____

_____

_____

_____

_____

_____

_____

_____

_____

_____

_____

_____

_____

_____

_____

_____

_____

Date _____

Medication _____   Adjustments _____

_____

Supplements _____

_____

Self-Care _____

_____

Best Thing That Happened Today _____

_____

Day of Cycle _____   Moon Phase_____

How I'm Feeling 1 2 3 4 5 6 7 8 9 10

_____

_____

_____

_____

_____

_____

_____

_____

_____

_____

_____

_____

_____

_____

_____

_____

_____

_____

_____

_____

_____

_____

_____

_____

_____

Date _____

Medication _____   Adjustments _____

_____

Supplements _____

_____

Self-Care _____

_____

Best Thing That Happened Today _____

_____

Day of Cycle _____   Moon Phase _____

How I'm Feeling 1 2 3 4 5 6 7 8 9 10

_____
_____
_____
_____
_____
_____
_____
_____
_____
_____
_____
_____
_____
_____
_____
_____
_____
_____
_____
_____
_____
_____
_____
_____
_____

Date _____

Medication _____   Adjustments _____

_____

Supplements _____

_____

Self-Care _____

_____

Best Thing That Happened Today _____

_____

Day of Cycle _____   Moon Phase _____

How I'm Feeling 1 2 3 4 5 6 7 8 9 10

_____

_____

_____

_____

_____

_____

_____

_____

_____

_____

_____

_____

_____

_____

_____

_____

_____

_____

_____

_____

_____

_____

_____

_____

Date _____

Medication _____   Adjustments _____

_____

Supplements _____

_____

Self-Care _____

_____

Best Thing That Happened Today _____

_____

Day of Cycle _____   Moon Phase _____

How I'm Feeling 1 2 3 4 5 6 7 8 9 10

_____

_____

_____

_____

_____

_____

_____

_____

_____

_____

_____

_____

_____

_____

_____

_____

_____

_____

_____

_____

_____

_____

_____

_____

_____

Date _____

Medication _____   Adjustments _____

_____

Supplements _____

_____

Self-Care _____

_____

Best Thing That Happened Today _____

_____

Day of Cycle _____   Moon Phase_____

How I'm Feeling 1 2 3 4 5 6 7 8 9 10

_____

_____

_____

_____

_____

_____

_____

_____

_____

_____

_____

_____

_____

_____

_____

_____

_____

_____

_____

_____

_____

_____

_____

_____

Date _____

Medication _____ Adjustments _____

_____

Supplements _____

_____

Self-Care _____

Best Thing That Happened Today _____

Day of Cycle _____ Moon Phase _____

How I'm Feeling 1 2 3 4 5 6 7 8 9 10

_____

_____

_____

_____

_____

_____

_____

_____

_____

_____

_____

_____

_____

_____

_____

_____

_____

_____

_____

_____

_____

_____

_____

_____

_____

_____

Date _____

Medication _____   Adjustments _____

_____

Supplements _____

_____

Self-Care _____

_____

Best Thing That Happened Today _____

_____

Day of Cycle _____   Moon Phase _____

How I'm Feeling 1 2 3 4 5 6 7 8 9 10

_____

_____

_____

_____

_____

_____

_____

_____

_____

_____

_____

_____

_____

_____

_____

_____

_____

_____

_____

_____

_____

_____

Date _____

Medication _____ Adjustments _____

_____

Supplements _____

_____

Self-Care _____

_____

Best Thing That Happened Today _____

_____

Day of Cycle _____ Moon Phase _____

How I'm Feeling 1 2 3 4 5 6 7 8 9 10

_____

_____

_____

_____

_____

_____

_____

_____

_____

_____

_____

_____

_____

_____

_____

_____

_____

_____

_____

_____

_____

_____

_____

_____

Date _____

Medication _____   Adjustments _____

_____

Supplements _____

_____

Self-Care _____

_____

Best Thing That Happened Today _____

_____

Day of Cycle _____   Moon Phase_____

How I'm Feeling 1 2 3 4 5 6 7 8 9 10

_____

_____

_____

_____

_____

_____

_____

_____

_____

_____

_____

_____

_____

_____

_____

_____

_____

_____

_____

_____

_____

_____

_____

Date _____

Medication _____   Adjustments _____

_____

Supplements _____

_____

Self-Care _____

_____

Best Thing That Happened Today _____

_____

Day of Cycle _____   Moon Phase _____

How I'm Feeling 1 2 3 4 5 6 7 8 9 10

_____
_____
_____
_____
_____
_____
_____
_____
_____
_____
_____
_____
_____
_____
_____
_____
_____
_____
_____
_____
_____
_____
_____
_____
_____

Date _____

Medication _____ Adjustments _____

_____

Supplements _____

_____

Self-Care _____

_____

Best Thing That Happened Today _____

_____

Day of Cycle _____ Moon Phase _____

How I'm Feeling 1 2 3 4 5 6 7 8 9 10

_____

_____

_____

_____

_____

_____

_____

_____

_____

_____

_____

_____

_____

_____

_____

_____

_____

_____

_____

_____

_____

_____

_____

_____

_____

_____

Date _____

Medication _____   Adjustments _____

_____

Supplements _____

_____

Self-Care _____

_____

Best Thing That Happened Today _____

_____

Day of Cycle _____   Moon Phase _____

How I'm Feeling 1 2 3 4 5 6 7 8 9 10

_____

_____

_____

_____

_____

_____

_____

_____

_____

_____

_____

_____

_____

_____

_____

_____

_____

_____

_____

_____

_____

Date ——————————

Medication _____   Adjustments _____

_____

Supplements _____

_____

Self-Care _____

_____

Best Thing That Happened Today _____

_____

Day of Cycle ——————   Moon Phase _____

How I'm Feeling 1 2 3 4 5 6 7 8 9 10

_____

_____

_____

_____

_____

_____

_____

_____

_____

_____

_____

_____

_____

_____

_____

_____

_____

_____

_____

_____

_____

_____

_____

Date _____

Medication_____ Adjustments _____

_____

Supplements _____

_____

Self-Care _____

_____

Best Thing That Happened Today _____

_____

Day of Cycle _____ Moon Phase_____

How I'm Feeling 1 2 3 4 5 6 7 8 9 10

_____

_____

_____

_____

_____

_____

_____

_____

_____

_____

_____

_____

_____

_____

_____

_____

_____

_____

_____

_____

_____

_____

_____

Date _____

Medication _____ Adjustments _____

_____

Supplements _____

_____

Self-Care _____

_____

Best Thing That Happened Today _____

_____

Day of Cycle _____ Moon Phase_____

How I'm Feeling 1 2 3 4 5 6 7 8 9 10

_____

_____

_____

_____

_____

_____

_____

_____

_____

_____

_____

_____

_____

_____

_____

_____

_____

_____

_____

_____

_____

_____

_____

_____

_____

Date _____

Medication _____   Adjustments _____

Supplements _____

Self-Care _____

Best Thing That Happened Today _____

Day of Cycle _____   Moon Phase _____

How I'm Feeling 1 2 3 4 5 6 7 8 9 10

_____
_____
_____
_____
_____
_____
_____
_____
_____
_____
_____
_____
_____
_____
_____
_____
_____
_____
_____
_____
_____
_____
_____
_____
_____

Date _____

Medication _____   Adjustments _____

_____

Supplements _____

_____

Self-Care _____

_____

Best Thing That Happened Today _____

_____

Day of Cycle _____   Moon Phase _____

How I'm Feeling 1 2 3 4 5 6 7 8 9 10

_____

_____

_____

_____

_____

_____

_____

_____

_____

_____

_____

_____

_____

_____

_____

_____

_____

_____

_____

_____

_____

_____

_____

Date _____

Medication _____   Adjustments _____

_____

Supplements _____

_____

Self-Care _____

_____

Best Thing That Happened Today _____

_____

Day of Cycle _____   Moon Phase _____

How I'm Feeling 1 2 3 4 5 6 7 8 9 10

_____

_____

_____

_____

_____

_____

_____

_____

_____

_____

_____

_____

_____

_____

_____

_____

_____

_____

_____

_____

_____

_____

_____

Date _____

Medication _____   Adjustments _____
_____

Supplements _____

Self-Care _____

Best Thing That Happened Today _____

Day of Cycle _____   Moon Phase _____

How I'm Feeling 1 2 3 4 5 6 7 8 9 10

_____

_____

_____

_____

_____

_____

_____

_____

_____

_____

_____

_____

_____

_____

_____

_____

_____

_____

_____

_____

_____

_____

_____

Date _____

Medication_____ Adjustments _____

_____

Supplements _____

_____

Self-Care _____

_____

Best Thing That Happened Today _____

_____

Day of Cycle _____ Moon Phase_____

How I'm Feeling 1 2 3 4 5 6 7 8 9 10

_____

_____

_____

_____

_____

_____

_____

_____

_____

_____

_____

_____

_____

_____

_____

_____

_____

_____

_____

_____

_____

_____

_____

_____

Date _____

Medication _____   Adjustments _____

_____

Supplements _____

_____

Self-Care _____

_____

Best Thing That Happened Today _____

_____

Day of Cycle _____   Moon Phase_____

How I'm Feeling 1 2 3 4 5 6 7 8 9 10

_____

_____

_____

_____

_____

_____

_____

_____

_____

_____

_____

_____

_____

_____

_____

_____

_____

_____

_____

_____

_____

_____

_____

_____

_____

Date _____

Medication_____   Adjustments _____

_____

Supplements _____

_____

Self-Care _____

_____

Best Thing That Happened Today _____

_____

Day of Cycle _____   Moon Phase_____

How I'm Feeling 1 2 3 4 5 6 7 8 9 10

_____

_____

_____

_____

_____

_____

_____

_____

_____

_____

_____

_____

_____

_____

_____

_____

_____

_____

_____

_____

_____

_____

_____

Date _____

Medication _____ Adjustments _____

_____

Supplements _____

_____

Self-Care _____

_____

Best Thing That Happened Today _____

_____

Day of Cycle _____ Moon Phase _____

How I'm Feeling 1 2 3 4 5 6 7 8 9 10

_____
_____
_____
_____
_____
_____
_____
_____
_____
_____
_____
_____
_____
_____
_____
_____
_____
_____
_____
_____
_____
_____
_____
_____
_____
_____

Date _____

Medication _____   Adjustments _____

_____

Supplements _____

_____

Self-Care _____

_____

Best Thing That Happened Today _____

_____

Day of Cycle _____   Moon Phase _____

How I'm Feeling   1 2 3 4 5 6 7 8 9 10

_____

_____

_____

_____

_____

_____

_____

_____

_____

_____

_____

_____

_____

_____

_____

_____

_____

_____

_____

_____

_____

_____

_____

Date _____

Medication _____   Adjustments _____

_____

Supplements _____

_____

Self-Care _____

_____

Best Thing That Happened Today _____

_____

Day of Cycle _____   Moon Phase _____

How I'm Feeling 1 2 3 4 5 6 7 8 9 10

_____

_____

_____

_____

_____

_____

_____

_____

_____

_____

_____

_____

_____

_____

_____

_____

_____

_____

_____

_____

_____

_____

_____

_____

Date _____

Medication_____ Adjustments _____

_____

Supplements _____

_____

Self-Care _____

_____

Best Thing That Happened Today _____

_____

Day of Cycle _____ Moon Phase_____

How I'm Feeling 1 2 3 4 5 6 7 8 9 10

_____

_____

_____

_____

_____

_____

_____

_____

_____

_____

_____

_____

_____

_____

_____

_____

_____

_____

_____

_____

_____

_____

_____

_____

_____

Date _____

Medication _____   Adjustments _____

_____

Supplements _____

_____

Self-Care _____

_____

Best Thing That Happened Today _____

_____

Day of Cycle _____   Moon Phase _____

How I'm Feeling 1 2 3 4 5 6 7 8 9 10

_____

_____

_____

_____

_____

_____

_____

_____

_____

_____

_____

_____

_____

_____

_____

_____

_____

_____

_____

_____

_____

_____

_____

_____

Date _____

Medication_____   Adjustments _____

_____

Supplements _____

_____

Self-Care _____

_____

Best Thing That Happened Today _____

_____

Day of Cycle _____   Moon Phase_____

How I'm Feeling 1 2 3 4 5 6 7 8 9 10

_____

_____

_____

_____

_____

_____

_____

_____

_____

_____

_____

_____

_____

_____

_____

_____

_____

_____

_____

_____

_____

_____

_____

Date _____

Medication _____   Adjustments _____

_____

Supplements _____

Self-Care _____

Best Thing That Happened Today _____

Day of Cycle _____   Moon Phase _____

How I'm Feeling 1 2 3 4 5 6 7 8 9 10

_____

_____

_____

_____

_____

_____

_____

_____

_____

_____

_____

_____

_____

_____

_____

_____

_____

_____

_____

_____

_____

_____

_____

_____

Date _____

Medication _____ Adjustments _____

_____

Supplements _____

_____

Self-Care _____

_____

Best Thing That Happened Today _____

_____

Day of Cycle _____ Moon Phase _____

How I'm Feeling 1 2 3 4 5 6 7 8 9 10

_____

_____

_____

_____

_____

_____

_____

_____

_____

_____

_____

_____

_____

_____

_____

_____

_____

_____

_____

_____

_____

_____

_____

_____

Date _____

Medication _____   Adjustments _____

_____

Supplements _____

_____

Self-Care _____

_____

Best Thing That Happened Today _____

_____

Day of Cycle _____   Moon Phase _____

How I'm Feeling 1 2 3 4 5 6 7 8 9 10

_____

_____

_____

_____

_____

_____

_____

_____

_____

_____

_____

_____

_____

_____

_____

_____

_____

_____

_____

_____

_____

_____

_____

Date _____

Medication _____ Adjustments _____

_____

Supplements _____

_____

Self-Care _____

_____

Best Thing That Happened Today _____

_____

Day of Cycle _____   Moon Phase _____

How I'm Feeling 1 2 3 4 5 6 7 8 9 10

_____

_____

_____

_____

_____

_____

_____

_____

_____

_____

_____

_____

_____

_____

_____

_____

_____

_____

_____

_____

_____

_____

_____

Date _____

Medication _____   Adjustments _____

_____

Supplements _____

_____

Self-Care _____

_____

Best Thing That Happened Today _____

_____

Day of Cycle _____   Moon Phase_____

How I'm Feeling 1 2 3 4 5 6 7 8 9 10

_____

_____

_____

_____

_____

_____

_____

_____

_____

_____

_____

_____

_____

_____

_____

_____

_____

_____

_____

_____

_____

_____

_____

_____

Date _____

Medication_____   Adjustments _____

_____

Supplements _____

_____

Self-Care _____

_____

Best Thing That Happened Today _____

_____

Day of Cycle _____   Moon Phase_____

How I'm Feeling 1 2 3 4 5 6 7 8 9 10

_____

_____

_____

_____

_____

_____

_____

_____

_____

_____

_____

_____

_____

_____

_____

_____

_____

_____

_____

_____

_____

_____

_____

_____

Date _____

Medication _____   Adjustments _____

_____

Supplements _____

_____

Self-Care _____

_____

Best Thing That Happened Today _____

_____

Day of Cycle _____   Moon Phase _____

How I'm Feeling 1 2 3 4 5 6 7 8 9 10

_____

_____

_____

_____

_____

_____

_____

_____

_____

_____

_____

_____

_____

_____

_____

_____

_____

_____

_____

_____

_____

_____

_____

_____

Date _____

Medication _____   Adjustments _____

_____

Supplements _____

_____

Self-Care _____

_____

Best Thing That Happened Today _____

_____

Day of Cycle _____   Moon Phase _____

How I'm Feeling   1 2 3 4 5 6 7 8 9 10

_____

_____

_____

_____

_____

_____

_____

_____

_____

_____

_____

_____

_____

_____

_____

_____

_____

_____

_____

_____

_____

_____

_____

_____

Date _____

Medication _____   Adjustments _____

_____

Supplements _____

_____

Self-Care _____

_____

Best Thing That Happened Today _____

_____

Day of Cycle _____   Moon Phase _____

How I'm Feeling 1 2 3 4 5 6 7 8 9 10

_____

_____

_____

_____

_____

_____

_____

_____

_____

_____

_____

_____

_____

_____

_____

_____

_____

_____

_____

_____

_____

_____

_____

Date _____

Medication _____ Adjustments _____

_____

Supplements _____

_____

Self-Care _____

_____

Best Thing That Happened Today _____

_____

Day of Cycle _____ Moon Phase _____

How I'm Feeling 1 2 3 4 5 6 7 8 9 10

_____

_____

_____

_____

_____

_____

_____

_____

_____

_____

_____

_____

_____

_____

_____

_____

_____

_____

_____

_____

_____

_____

_____

_____

_____

Date _____

Medication _____   Adjustments _____

_____

Supplements _____

_____

Self-Care _____

_____

Best Thing That Happened Today _____

_____

Day of Cycle _____   Moon Phase_____

How I'm Feeling 1 2 3 4 5 6 7 8 9 10

_____

_____

_____

_____

_____

_____

_____

_____

_____

_____

_____

_____

_____

_____

_____

_____

_____

_____

_____

_____

_____

_____

_____

_____

Date _____

Medication _____ Adjustments _____

_____

Supplements _____

_____

Self-Care _____

_____

Best Thing That Happened Today _____

_____

Day of Cycle _____ Moon Phase _____

How I'm Feeling 1 2 3 4 5 6 7 8 9 10

_____

_____

_____

_____

_____

_____

_____

_____

_____

_____

_____

_____

_____

_____

_____

_____

_____

_____

_____

_____

_____

_____

_____

_____

Date _____

Medication _____ Adjustments _____

_____

Supplements _____

_____

Self-Care _____

_____

Best Thing That Happened Today _____

_____

Day of Cycle _____ Moon Phase _____

How I'm Feeling 1 2 3 4 5 6 7 8 9 10

Date _____

Medication _____   Adjustments _____

_____

Supplements _____

_____

Self-Care _____

_____

Best Thing That Happened Today _____

_____

Day of Cycle _____   Moon Phase _____

How I'm Feeling 1 2 3 4 5 6 7 8 9 10

_____

_____

_____

_____

_____

_____

_____

_____

_____

_____

_____

_____

_____

_____

_____

_____

_____

_____

_____

_____

_____

_____

_____

Date _____

Medication _____   Adjustments _____

_____

Supplements _____

_____

Self-Care _____

_____

Best Thing That Happened Today _____

_____

Day of Cycle _____   Moon Phase _____

How I'm Feeling 1 2 3 4 5 6 7 8 9 10

_____

_____

_____

_____

_____

_____

_____

_____

_____

_____

_____

_____

_____

_____

_____

_____

_____

_____

_____

_____

_____

_____

_____

Date _____

Medication _____   Adjustments _____

_____

Supplements _____

_____

Self-Care _____

_____

Best Thing That Happened Today _____

_____

Day of Cycle _____   Moon Phase _____

How I'm Feeling 1 2 3 4 5 6 7 8 9 10

_____

_____

_____

_____

_____

_____

_____

_____

_____

_____

_____

_____

_____

_____

_____

_____

_____

_____

_____

_____

_____

_____

_____

Date _____

Medication _____   Adjustments _____

_____

Supplements _____

_____

Self-Care _____

_____

Best Thing That Happened Today _____

_____

Day of Cycle _____   Moon Phase _____

How I'm Feeling 1 2 3 4 5 6 7 8 9 10

_____

_____

_____

_____

_____

_____

_____

_____

_____

_____

_____

_____

_____

_____

_____

_____

_____

_____

_____

_____

_____

_____

_____

_____

Date _____

Medication _____   Adjustments _____

_____

Supplements _____

_____

Self-Care _____

_____

Best Thing That Happened Today _____

_____

Day of Cycle _____   Moon Phase _____

How I'm Feeling 1 2 3 4 5 6 7 8 9 10

_____

_____

_____

_____

_____

_____

_____

_____

_____

_____

_____

_____

_____

_____

_____

_____

_____

_____

_____

_____

_____

_____

_____

_____

Date _____

Medication _____   Adjustments _____

_____

Supplements _____

_____

Self-Care _____

_____

Best Thing That Happened Today _____

_____

Day of Cycle _____   Moon Phase _____

How I'm Feeling 1 2 3 4 5 6 7 8 9 10

_____

_____

_____

_____

_____

_____

_____

_____

_____

_____

_____

_____

_____

_____

_____

_____

_____

_____

_____

_____

_____

_____

_____

_____

Date _____

Medication _____   Adjustments _____

_____

Supplements _____

_____

Self-Care _____

_____

Best Thing That Happened Today _____

_____

Day of Cycle _____   Moon Phase _____

How I'm Feeling 1 2 3 4 5 6 7 8 9 10

_____

_____

_____

_____

_____

_____

_____

_____

_____

_____

_____

_____

_____

_____

_____

_____

_____

_____

_____

_____

_____

Date _____

Medication _____   Adjustments _____

_____

Supplements _____

_____

Self-Care _____

_____

Best Thing That Happened Today _____

_____

Day of Cycle _____   Moon Phase _____

How I'm Feeling 1 2 3 4 5 6 7 8 9 10

_____

_____

_____

_____

_____

_____

_____

_____

_____

_____

_____

_____

_____

_____

_____

_____

_____

_____

_____

_____

_____

_____

_____

_____

Date _____

Medication _____ Adjustments _____

_____

Supplements _____

_____

Self-Care _____

_____

Best Thing That Happened Today _____

_____

Day of Cycle _____ Moon Phase _____

How I'm Feeling 1 2 3 4 5 6 7 8 9 10

_____
_____
_____
_____
_____
_____
_____
_____
_____
_____
_____
_____
_____
_____
_____
_____
_____
_____
_____
_____
_____
_____
_____
_____
_____
_____
_____

Date _____

Medication _____   Adjustments _____

_____

Supplements _____

_____

Self-Care _____

_____

Best Thing That Happened Today _____

_____

Day of Cycle _____   Moon Phase _____

How I'm Feeling 1 2 3 4 5 6 7 8 9 10

_____

_____

_____

_____

_____

_____

_____

_____

_____

_____

_____

_____

_____

_____

_____

_____

_____

_____

_____

_____

_____

_____

Date _____

Medication _____ Adjustments _____

_____

Supplements _____

_____

Self-Care _____

_____

Best Thing That Happened Today _____

_____

Day of Cycle _____ Moon Phase _____

How I'm Feeling 1 2 3 4 5 6 7 8 9 10

_____

_____

_____

_____

_____

_____

_____

_____

_____

_____

_____

_____

_____

_____

_____

_____

_____

_____

_____

_____

_____

_____

_____

_____

_____

Date _____

Medication _____ Adjustments _____

_____

Supplements _____

_____

Self-Care _____

_____

Best Thing That Happened Today _____

_____

Day of Cycle _____ Moon Phase _____

How I'm Feeling 1 2 3 4 5 6 7 8 9 10

_____

_____

_____

_____

_____

_____

_____

_____

_____

_____

_____

_____

_____

_____

_____

_____

_____

_____

_____

_____

_____

_____

_____

Date _____

Medication _____ Adjustments _____

_____

Supplements _____

_____

Self-Care _____

_____

Best Thing That Happened Today _____

_____

Day of Cycle _____ Moon Phase _____

How I'm Feeling 1 2 3 4 5 6 7 8 9 10

_____

_____

_____

_____

_____

_____

_____

_____

_____

_____

_____

_____

_____

_____

_____

_____

_____

_____

_____

_____

_____

_____

_____

_____

_____

Date _____

Medication _____   Adjustments _____
_____

Supplements _____

Self-Care _____

Best Thing That Happened Today _____

Day of Cycle _____   Moon Phase _____

How I'm Feeling 1 2 3 4 5 6 7 8 9 10

_____
_____
_____
_____
_____
_____
_____
_____
_____
_____
_____
_____
_____
_____
_____
_____
_____
_____
_____
_____
_____
_____
_____
_____

Date _____

Medication _____ Adjustments _____

_____

Supplements _____

_____

Self-Care _____

_____

Best Thing That Happened Today _____

_____

Day of Cycle _____ Moon Phase _____

How I'm Feeling 1 2 3 4 5 6 7 8 9 10

_____

_____

_____

_____

_____

_____

_____

_____

_____

_____

_____

_____

_____

_____

_____

_____

_____

_____

_____

_____

_____

_____

_____

_____

Date _____

Medication _____   Adjustments _____

_____

Supplements _____

_____

Self-Care _____

_____

Best Thing That Happened Today _____

_____

Day of Cycle _____   Moon Phase _____

How I'm Feeling 1 2 3 4 5 6 7 8 9 10

_____

_____

_____

_____

_____

_____

_____

_____

_____

_____

_____

_____

_____

_____

_____

_____

_____

_____

_____

_____

_____

_____

_____

_____

_____

Date _____

Medication _____   Adjustments _____

_____

Supplements _____

_____

Self-Care _____

_____

Best Thing That Happened Today _____

_____

Day of Cycle _____   Moon Phase _____

How I'm Feeling 1 2 3 4 5 6 7 8 9 10

_____

_____

_____

_____

_____

_____

_____

_____

_____

_____

_____

_____

_____

_____

_____

_____

_____

_____

_____

_____

_____

_____

_____

_____

_____

Date _____

Medication _____   Adjustments _____

_____

Supplements _____

_____

Self-Care _____

_____

Best Thing That Happened Today _____

_____

Day of Cycle _____   Moon Phase _____

How I'm Feeling 1 2 3 4 5 6 7 8 9 10

_____

_____

_____

_____

_____

_____

_____

_____

_____

_____

_____

_____

_____

_____

_____

_____

_____

_____

_____

_____

_____

_____

_____

_____

Date _____

Medication _____ Adjustments _____

_____

Supplements _____

_____

Self-Care _____

_____

Best Thing That Happened Today _____

_____

Day of Cycle _____ Moon Phase _____

How I'm Feeling 1 2 3 4 5 6 7 8 9 10

_____

_____

_____

_____

_____

_____

_____

_____

_____

_____

_____

_____

_____

_____

_____

_____

_____

_____

_____

_____

_____

Date _____

Medication _____   Adjustments _____

_____

Supplements _____

_____

Self-Care _____

_____

Best Thing That Happened Today _____

_____

Day of Cycle _____   Moon Phase _____

How I'm Feeling 1 2 3 4 5 6 7 8 9 10

_____

_____

_____

_____

_____

_____

_____

_____

_____

_____

_____

_____

_____

_____

_____

_____

_____

_____

_____

_____

_____

_____

_____

_____

Date _____

Medication _____   Adjustments _____

_____

Supplements _____

_____

Self-Care _____

_____

Best Thing That Happened Today _____

_____

Day of Cycle _____   Moon Phase _____

How I'm Feeling 1 2 3 4 5 6 7 8 9 10

_____

_____

_____

_____

_____

_____

_____

_____

_____

_____

_____

_____

_____

_____

_____

_____

_____

_____

_____

_____

_____

_____

_____

_____

_____

Date _____

Medication _____ Adjustments _____

Supplements _____

Self-Care _____

Best Thing That Happened Today _____

Day of Cycle _____ Moon Phase _____

How I'm Feeling 1 2 3 4 5 6 7 8 9 10

_____

_____

_____

_____

_____

_____

_____

_____

_____

_____

_____

_____

_____

_____

_____

_____

_____

_____

_____

_____

_____

Date _____

Medication _____ Adjustments _____

_____

Supplements _____

_____

Self-Care _____

_____

Best Thing That Happened Today _____

_____

Day of Cycle _____ Moon Phase _____

How I'm Feeling 1 2 3 4 5 6 7 8 9 10

_____

_____

_____

_____

_____

_____

_____

_____

_____

_____

_____

_____

_____

_____

_____

_____

_____

_____

_____

_____

_____

_____

_____

_____

Date _____

Medication _____ Adjustments _____

_____

Supplements _____

_____

Self-Care _____

_____

Best Thing That Happened Today _____

_____

Day of Cycle _____ Moon Phase _____

How I'm Feeling 1 2 3 4 5 6 7 8 9 10

_____

_____

_____

_____

_____

_____

_____

_____

_____

_____

_____

_____

_____

_____

_____

_____

_____

_____

_____

_____

_____

_____

_____

Date _____

Medication _____   Adjustments _____

_____

Supplements _____

_____

Self-Care _____

_____

Best Thing That Happened Today _____

_____

Day of Cycle _____   Moon Phase _____

How I'm Feeling 1 2 3 4 5 6 7 8 9 10

_____

_____

_____

_____

_____

_____

_____

_____

_____

_____

_____

_____

_____

_____

_____

_____

_____

_____

_____

_____

_____

_____

_____

_____

Date _____

Medication _____   Adjustments _____

_____

Supplements _____

_____

Self-Care _____

_____

Best Thing That Happened Today _____

_____

Day of Cycle _____   Moon Phase _____

How I'm Feeling 1 2 3 4 5 6 7 8 9 10

_____

_____

_____

_____

_____

_____

_____

_____

_____

_____

_____

_____

_____

_____

_____

_____

_____

_____

_____

_____

_____

_____

_____

_____

Date _____

Medication _____   Adjustments _____

_____

Supplements _____

_____

Self-Care _____

_____

Best Thing That Happened Today _____

_____

Day of Cycle _____   Moon Phase _____

How I'm Feeling 1 2 3 4 5 6 7 8 9 10

_____
_____
_____
_____
_____
_____
_____
_____
_____
_____
_____
_____
_____
_____
_____
_____
_____
_____
_____
_____
_____
_____
_____
_____
_____
_____

Date _____

Medication _____   Adjustments _____
_____

Supplements _____

_____

Self-Care _____

_____

Best Thing That Happened Today _____

_____

Day of Cycle _____   Moon Phase _____

How I'm Feeling 1 2 3 4 5 6 7 8 9 10

_____

_____

_____

_____

_____

_____

_____

_____

_____

_____

_____

_____

_____

_____

_____

_____

_____

_____

_____

_____

_____

_____

Date _____

Medication _____   Adjustments _____

_____

Supplements _____

_____

Self-Care _____

_____

Best Thing That Happened Today _____

_____

Day of Cycle _____   Moon Phase _____

How I'm Feeling 1 2 3 4 5 6 7 8 9 10

_____

_____

_____

_____

_____

_____

_____

_____

_____

_____

_____

_____

_____

_____

_____

_____

_____

_____

_____

_____

_____

_____

_____

_____

_____

Date _____

Medication _____   Adjustments _____
_____

Supplements _____
_____

Self-Care _____
_____

Best Thing That Happened Today _____
_____

Day of Cycle _____   Moon Phase_____

How I'm Feeling 1 2 3 4 5 6 7 8 9 10

_____
_____
_____
_____
_____
_____
_____
_____
_____
_____
_____
_____
_____
_____
_____
_____
_____
_____
_____
_____
_____
_____
_____
_____

Date _____

Medication _____ Adjustments _____

_____

Supplements _____

_____

Self-Care _____

_____

Best Thing That Happened Today _____

_____

Day of Cycle _____ Moon Phase _____

How I'm Feeling 1 2 3 4 5 6 7 8 9 10

_____
_____
_____
_____
_____
_____
_____
_____
_____
_____
_____
_____
_____
_____
_____
_____
_____
_____
_____
_____
_____
_____
_____

Date _____

Medication _____   Adjustments _____

_____

Supplements _____

_____

Self-Care _____

_____

Best Thing That Happened Today _____

_____

Day of Cycle _____   Moon Phase_____

How I'm Feeling 1 2 3 4 5 6 7 8 9 10

_____

_____

_____

_____

_____

_____

_____

_____

_____

_____

_____

_____

_____

_____

_____

_____

_____

_____

_____

_____

_____

_____

Date _____

Medication _____ Adjustments _____

_____

Supplements _____

_____

Self-Care _____

_____

Best Thing That Happened Today _____

_____

Day of Cycle _____ Moon Phase _____

How I'm Feeling 1 2 3 4 5 6 7 8 9 10

_____
_____
_____
_____
_____
_____
_____
_____
_____
_____
_____
_____
_____
_____
_____
_____
_____
_____
_____
_____
_____
_____
_____
_____
_____
_____

Date _____

Medication _____   Adjustments _____

_____

Supplements _____

_____

Self-Care _____

_____

Best Thing That Happened Today _____

_____

Day of Cycle _____   Moon Phase_____

How I'm Feeling 1 2 3 4 5 6 7 8 9 10

_____

_____

_____

_____

_____

_____

_____

_____

_____

_____

_____

_____

_____

_____

_____

_____

_____

_____

_____

_____

_____

_____

_____

_____

Date _____

Medication_____   Adjustments _____

_____

Supplements _____

_____

Self-Care _____

_____

Best Thing That Happened Today _____

_____

Day of Cycle _____   Moon Phase_____

How I'm Feeling 1 2 3 4 5 6 7 8 9 10

_____

_____

_____

_____

_____

_____

_____

_____

_____

_____

_____

_____

_____

_____

_____

_____

_____

_____

_____

_____

_____

_____

_____

_____

_____

Date _____

Medication _____   Adjustments _____

_____

Supplements _____

_____

Self-Care _____

_____

Best Thing That Happened Today _____

_____

Day of Cycle _____   Moon Phase _____

How I'm Feeling 1 2 3 4 5 6 7 8 9 10

_____

_____

_____

_____

_____

_____

_____

_____

_____

_____

_____

_____

_____

_____

_____

_____

_____

_____

_____

_____

_____

_____

_____

_____

Date _____

Medication _____   Adjustments _____

_____

Supplements _____

_____

Self-Care _____

_____

Best Thing That Happened Today _____

_____

Day of Cycle _____   Moon Phase _____

How I'm Feeling 1 2 3 4 5 6 7 8 9 10

_____

_____

_____

_____

_____

_____

_____

_____

_____

_____

_____

_____

_____

_____

_____

_____

_____

_____

_____

_____

_____

Date _____

Medication _____ Adjustments _____

_____

Supplements _____

_____

Self-Care _____

_____

Best Thing That Happened Today _____

_____

Day of Cycle _____ Moon Phase _____

How I'm Feeling 1 2 3 4 5 6 7 8 9 10

_____

_____

_____

_____

_____

_____

_____

_____

_____

_____

_____

_____

_____

_____

_____

_____

_____

_____

_____

_____

_____

_____

_____

_____

Date _____

Medication _____   Adjustments _____

_____

Supplements _____

_____

Self-Care _____

Best Thing That Happened Today _____

Day of Cycle _____   Moon Phase _____

How I'm Feeling 1 2 3 4 5 6 7 8 9 10

_____

_____

_____

_____

_____

_____

_____

_____

_____

_____

_____

_____

_____

_____

_____

_____

_____

_____

_____

_____

_____

_____

_____

_____

Date _____

Medication _____   Adjustments _____

_____

Supplements _____

_____

Self-Care _____

_____

Best Thing That Happened Today _____

_____

Day of Cycle _____   Moon Phase _____

How I'm Feeling 1 2 3 4 5 6 7 8 9 10

_____

_____

_____

_____

_____

_____

_____

_____

_____

_____

_____

_____

_____

_____

_____

_____

_____

_____

_____

_____

_____

_____

_____

_____

_____

Date _____

Medication _____   Adjustments _____

_____

Supplements _____

_____

Self-Care _____

_____

Best Thing That Happened Today _____

_____

Day of Cycle _____   Moon Phase _____

How I'm Feeling 1 2 3 4 5 6 7 8 9 10

_____

_____

_____

_____

_____

_____

_____

_____

_____

_____

_____

_____

_____

_____

_____

_____

_____

_____

_____

_____

_____

_____

_____

_____

_____

_____

Date _____

Medication _____   Adjustments _____

_____

Supplements _____

_____

Self-Care _____

_____

Best Thing That Happened Today _____

_____

Day of Cycle _____   Moon Phase_____

How I'm Feeling 1 2 3 4 5 6 7 8 9 10

_____

_____

_____

_____

_____

_____

_____

_____

_____

_____

_____

_____

_____

_____

_____

_____

_____

_____

_____

_____

_____

_____

_____

_____

Date _____

Medication _____   Adjustments _____

_____

Supplements _____

_____

Self-Care _____

_____

Best Thing That Happened Today _____

_____

Day of Cycle _____   Moon Phase _____

How I'm Feeling 1 2 3 4 5 6 7 8 9 10

_____

_____

_____

_____

_____

_____

_____

_____

_____

_____

_____

_____

_____

_____

_____

_____

_____

_____

_____

_____

_____

_____

_____

Date _____

Medication _____   Adjustments _____
_____

Supplements _____
_____

Self-Care _____
_____

Best Thing That Happened Today _____
_____

Day of Cycle _____   Moon Phase _____

How I'm Feeling 1 2 3 4 5 6 7 8 9 10

_____
_____
_____
_____
_____
_____
_____
_____
_____
_____
_____
_____
_____
_____
_____
_____
_____
_____
_____
_____
_____
_____
_____
_____
_____

Date _____

Medication _____   Adjustments _____

_____

Supplements _____

_____

Self-Care _____

_____

Best Thing That Happened Today _____

_____

Day of Cycle _____   Moon Phase _____

How I'm Feeling 1 2 3 4 5 6 7 8 9 10

_____

_____

_____

_____

_____

_____

_____

_____

_____

_____

_____

_____

_____

_____

_____

_____

_____

_____

_____

_____

_____

_____

_____

_____

_____

_____

Date _____

Medication _____   Adjustments _____

_____

Supplements _____

_____

Self-Care _____

_____

Best Thing That Happened Today _____

_____

Day of Cycle _____   Moon Phase _____

How I'm Feeling 1 2 3 4 5 6 7 8 9 10

_____

_____

_____

_____

_____

_____

_____

_____

_____

_____

_____

_____

_____

_____

_____

_____

_____

_____

_____

_____

_____

_____

_____

_____

_____

Date _____

Medication _____ Adjustments _____

_____

Supplements _____

_____

Self-Care _____

Best Thing That Happened Today _____

Day of Cycle _____ Moon Phase _____

How I'm Feeling 1 2 3 4 5 6 7 8 9 10

_____

_____

_____

_____

_____

_____

_____

_____

_____

_____

_____

_____

_____

_____

_____

_____

_____

_____

_____

_____

_____

_____

_____

_____

_____

_____

Date _____

Medication _____   Adjustments _____

_____

Supplements _____

_____

Self-Care _____

_____

Best Thing That Happened Today _____

_____

Day of Cycle _____   Moon Phase _____

How I'm Feeling 1 2 3 4 5 6 7 8 9 10

_____

_____

_____

_____

_____

_____

_____

_____

_____

_____

_____

_____

_____

_____

_____

_____

_____

_____

_____

_____

_____

_____

_____

_____

Date _____

Medication _____   Adjustments _____

_____

Supplements _____

_____

Self-Care _____

_____

Best Thing That Happened Today _____

_____

Day of Cycle _____   Moon Phase _____

How I'm Feeling 1 2 3 4 5 6 7 8 9 10

_____

_____

_____

_____

_____

_____

_____

_____

_____

_____

_____

_____

_____

_____

_____

_____

_____

_____

_____

_____

_____

Date _____

Medication _____   Adjustments _____

_____

Supplements _____

_____

Self-Care _____

_____

Best Thing That Happened Today _____

_____

Day of Cycle _____   Moon Phase _____

How I'm Feeling 1 2 3 4 5 6 7 8 9 10

_____

_____

_____

_____

_____

_____

_____

_____

_____

_____

_____

_____

_____

_____

_____

_____

_____

_____

_____

_____

_____

_____

_____

Date _____

Medication _____   Adjustments _____

_____

Supplements _____

_____

Self-Care _____

_____

Best Thing That Happened Today _____

_____

Day of Cycle _____   Moon Phase _____

How I'm Feeling 1 2 3 4 5 6 7 8 9 10

_____
_____
_____
_____
_____
_____
_____
_____
_____
_____
_____
_____
_____
_____
_____
_____
_____
_____
_____
_____
_____
_____
_____
_____
_____
_____

Date _____

Medication _____   Adjustments _____

_____

Supplements _____

_____

Self-Care _____

_____

Best Thing That Happened Today _____

_____

Day of Cycle _____   Moon Phase _____

How I'm Feeling 1 2 3 4 5 6 7 8 9 10

_____

_____

_____

_____

_____

_____

_____

_____

_____

_____

_____

_____

_____

_____

_____

_____

_____

_____

_____

_____

_____

_____

_____

Date _____

Medication_____   Adjustments _____
_____

Supplements _____
_____

Self-Care _____
_____

Best Thing That Happened Today _____
_____

Day of Cycle _____   Moon Phase_____

How I'm Feeling 1 2 3 4 5 6 7 8 9 10

_____

_____

_____

_____

_____

_____

_____

_____

_____

_____

_____

_____

_____

_____

_____

_____

_____

_____

_____

_____

_____

_____

_____

_____

Date _____

Medication _____   Adjustments _____

_____

Supplements _____

_____

Self-Care _____

_____

Best Thing That Happened Today _____

_____

Day of Cycle _____   Moon Phase_____

How I'm Feeling 1 2 3 4 5 6 7 8 9 10

_____

_____

_____

_____

_____

_____

_____

_____

_____

_____

_____

_____

_____

_____

_____

_____

_____

_____

_____

_____

_____

_____

_____

_____

_____

_____

Date _____

Medication _____   Adjustments _____

_____

Supplements _____

_____

Self-Care _____

_____

Best Thing That Happened Today _____

_____

Day of Cycle _____   Moon Phase _____

How I'm Feeling 1 2 3 4 5 6 7 8 9 10

_____

_____

_____

_____

_____

_____

_____

_____

_____

_____

_____

_____

_____

_____

_____

_____

_____

_____

_____

_____

_____

_____

_____

Date _____

Medication _____   Adjustments _____

_____

Supplements _____

_____

Self-Care _____

_____

Best Thing That Happened Today _____

_____

Day of Cycle _____   Moon Phase _____

How I'm Feeling 1 2 3 4 5 6 7 8 9 10

_____
_____
_____
_____
_____
_____
_____
_____
_____
_____
_____
_____
_____
_____
_____
_____
_____
_____
_____
_____
_____
_____
_____

Date _____

Medication _____   Adjustments _____

_____

Supplements _____

_____

Self-Care _____

_____

Best Thing That Happened Today _____

_____

Day of Cycle _____   Moon Phase _____

How I'm Feeling 1 2 3 4 5 6 7 8 9 10

_____
_____
_____
_____
_____
_____
_____
_____
_____
_____
_____
_____
_____
_____
_____
_____
_____
_____
_____
_____
_____
_____
_____
_____
_____

Date _____

Medication _____   Adjustments _____

_____

Supplements _____

_____

Self-Care _____

_____

Best Thing That Happened Today _____

_____

Day of Cycle _____   Moon Phase_____

How I'm Feeling 1 2 3 4 5 6 7 8 9 10

_____

_____

_____

_____

_____

_____

_____

_____

_____

_____

_____

_____

_____

_____

_____

_____

_____

_____

_____

_____

_____

_____

_____

_____

_____

Date _____

Medication _____   Adjustments _____

_____

Supplements _____

_____

Self-Care _____

_____

Best Thing That Happened Today _____

_____

Day of Cycle _____   Moon Phase _____

How I'm Feeling 1 2 3 4 5 6 7 8 9 10

_____

_____

_____

_____

_____

_____

_____

_____

_____

_____

_____

_____

_____

_____

_____

_____

_____

_____

_____

_____

_____

_____

_____

_____

_____

Date _____

Medication _____   Adjustments _____

_____

Supplements _____

_____

Self-Care _____

_____

Best Thing That Happened Today _____

_____

Day of Cycle _____   Moon Phase _____

How I'm Feeling 1 2 3 4 5 6 7 8 9 10

_____

_____

_____

_____

_____

_____

_____

_____

_____

_____

_____

_____

_____

_____

_____

_____

_____

_____

_____

_____

_____

_____

_____

_____

Date _____

Medication _____   Adjustments _____

_____

Supplements _____

_____

Self-Care _____

_____

Best Thing That Happened Today _____

_____

Day of Cycle _____   Moon Phase _____

How I'm Feeling 1 2 3 4 5 6 7 8 9 10

_____

_____

_____

_____

_____

_____

_____

_____

_____

_____

_____

_____

_____

_____

_____

_____

_____

_____

_____

_____

_____

_____

_____

_____

Date _____

Medication _____   Adjustments _____
_____

Supplements _____
_____

Self-Care _____
_____

Best Thing That Happened Today _____
_____

Day of Cycle _____   Moon Phase _____

How I'm Feeling 1 2 3 4 5 6 7 8 9 10

_____
_____
_____
_____
_____
_____
_____
_____
_____
_____
_____
_____
_____
_____
_____
_____
_____
_____
_____
_____
_____
_____

Date _____

Medication _____   Adjustments _____

_____

Supplements _____

_____

Self-Care _____

_____

Best Thing That Happened Today _____

_____

Day of Cycle _____   Moon Phase _____

How I'm Feeling 1 2 3 4 5 6 7 8 9 10

_____

_____

_____

_____

_____

_____

_____

_____

_____

_____

_____

_____

_____

_____

_____

_____

_____

_____

_____

_____

_____

_____

_____

_____

_____

_____

Date _____

Medication _____   Adjustments _____

_____

Supplements _____

_____

Self-Care _____

_____

Best Thing That Happened Today _____

_____

Day of Cycle _____   Moon Phase_____

How I'm Feeling 1 2 3 4 5 6 7 8 9 10

_____

_____

_____

_____

_____

_____

_____

_____

_____

_____

_____

_____

_____

_____

_____

_____

_____

_____

_____

_____

_____

_____

_____

Date _____

Medication _____   Adjustments _____

_____

Supplements _____

_____

Self-Care _____

_____

Best Thing That Happened Today _____

_____

Day of Cycle _____   Moon Phase _____

How I'm Feeling 1 2 3 4 5 6 7 8 9 10

_____

_____

_____

_____

_____

_____

_____

_____

_____

_____

_____

_____

_____

_____

_____

_____

_____

_____

_____

_____

_____

_____

_____

_____

Date _____

Medication _____   Adjustments _____
_____

Supplements _____

Self-Care _____
_____

Best Thing That Happened Today _____
_____

Day of Cycle _____   Moon Phase _____

How I'm Feeling 1 2 3 4 5 6 7 8 9 10

_____
_____
_____
_____
_____
_____
_____
_____
_____
_____
_____
_____
_____
_____
_____
_____
_____
_____
_____
_____
_____
_____
_____
_____
_____
_____

Date _____

Medication _____   Adjustments _____

_____

Supplements _____

_____

Self-Care _____

_____

Best Thing That Happened Today _____

_____

Day of Cycle _____   Moon Phase _____

How I'm Feeling 1 2 3 4 5 6 7 8 9 10

_____

_____

_____

_____

_____

_____

_____

_____

_____

_____

_____

_____

_____

_____

_____

_____

_____

_____

_____

_____

_____

_____

_____

_____

Date _____

Medication _____   Adjustments _____

_____

Supplements _____

_____

Self-Care _____

_____

Best Thing That Happened Today _____

_____

Day of Cycle _____   Moon Phase _____

How I'm Feeling 1 2 3 4 5 6 7 8 9 10

_____

_____

_____

_____

_____

_____

_____

_____

_____

_____

_____

_____

_____

_____

_____

_____

_____

_____

_____

_____

_____

_____

_____

_____

_____

Date _____

Medication _____ Adjustments _____

_____

Supplements _____

_____

Self-Care _____

_____

Best Thing That Happened Today _____

_____

Day of Cycle _____   Moon Phase _____

How I'm Feeling 1 2 3 4 5 6 7 8 9 10

_____

_____

_____

_____

_____

_____

_____

_____

_____

_____

_____

_____

_____

_____

_____

_____

_____

_____

_____

_____

_____

_____

_____

_____

Date _____

Medication _____   Adjustments _____
_____

Supplements _____
_____

Self-Care _____

Best Thing That Happened Today _____
_____

Day of Cycle _____   Moon Phase _____

How I'm Feeling 1 2 3 4 5 6 7 8 9 10

_____
_____
_____
_____
_____
_____
_____
_____
_____
_____
_____
_____
_____
_____
_____
_____
_____
_____
_____
_____
_____
_____
_____
_____
_____

Date _____

Medication _____   Adjustments _____
_____

Supplements _____
_____

Self-Care _____

Best Thing That Happened Today _____
_____

Day of Cycle _____   Moon Phase _____

How I'm Feeling 1 2 3 4 5 6 7 8 9 10

_____
_____
_____
_____
_____
_____
_____
_____
_____
_____
_____
_____
_____
_____
_____
_____
_____
_____
_____
_____
_____
_____
_____
_____
_____

Date _____

Medication _____   Adjustments _____
_____

Supplements _____
_____

Self-Care _____
_____

Best Thing That Happened Today _____
_____

Day of Cycle _____   Moon Phase _____

How I'm Feeling 1 2 3 4 5 6 7 8 9 10

_____
_____
_____
_____
_____
_____
_____
_____
_____
_____
_____
_____
_____
_____
_____
_____
_____
_____
_____
_____
_____
_____
_____
_____
_____

Date _____

Medication _____   Adjustments _____
_____

Supplements _____
_____

Self-Care _____
_____

Best Thing That Happened Today _____
_____

Day of Cycle _____   Moon Phase _____

How I'm Feeling 1 2 3 4 5 6 7 8 9 10

_____
_____
_____
_____
_____
_____
_____
_____
_____
_____
_____
_____
_____
_____
_____
_____
_____
_____
_____
_____
_____
_____
_____

Date _____

Medication _____ Adjustments _____

_____

Supplements _____

_____

Self-Care _____

_____

Best Thing That Happened Today _____

_____

Day of Cycle _____ Moon Phase _____

How I'm Feeling 1 2 3 4 5 6 7 8 9 10

_____

_____

_____

_____

_____

_____

_____

_____

_____

_____

_____

_____

_____

_____

_____

_____

_____

_____

_____

_____

_____

_____

_____

_____

_____

Date _____

Medication _____   Adjustments _____

_____

Supplements _____

_____

Self-Care _____

_____

Best Thing That Happened Today _____

_____

Day of Cycle _____   Moon Phase _____

How I'm Feeling 1 2 3 4 5 6 7 8 9 10

_____

_____

_____

_____

_____

_____

_____

_____

_____

_____

_____

_____

_____

_____

_____

_____

_____

_____

_____

_____

_____

_____

_____

_____

Date _____

Medication _____   Adjustments _____
_____

Supplements _____
_____

Self-Care _____
_____

Best Thing That Happened Today _____
_____

Day of Cycle _____   Moon Phase _____

How I'm Feeling 1 2 3 4 5 6 7 8 9 10

_____
_____
_____
_____
_____
_____
_____
_____
_____
_____
_____
_____
_____
_____
_____
_____
_____
_____
_____
_____
_____
_____
_____
_____

Date _____

Medication_____   Adjustments _____

_____

Supplements _____

_____

Self-Care _____

_____

Best Thing That Happened Today _____

_____

Day of Cycle _____   Moon Phase_____

How I'm Feeling 1 2 3 4 5 6 7 8 9 10

_____

_____

_____

_____

_____

_____

_____

_____

_____

_____

_____

_____

_____

_____

_____

_____

_____

_____

_____

_____

_____

_____

_____

Date _____

Medication _____   Adjustments _____

_____

Supplements _____

_____

Self-Care _____

_____

Best Thing That Happened Today _____

_____

Day of Cycle _____   Moon Phase _____

How I'm Feeling 1 2 3 4 5 6 7 8 9 10

_____

_____

_____

_____

_____

_____

_____

_____

_____

_____

_____

_____

_____

_____

_____

_____

_____

_____

_____

_____

_____

_____

_____

_____

Date _____

Medication _____   Adjustments _____
_____

Supplements _____
_____

Self-Care _____
_____

Best Thing That Happened Today _____
_____

Day of Cycle _____   Moon Phase _____

How I'm Feeling 1 2 3 4 5 6 7 8 9 10

_____
_____
_____
_____
_____
_____
_____
_____
_____
_____
_____
_____
_____
_____
_____
_____
_____
_____
_____
_____
_____
_____
_____
_____

Date _____

Medication _____   Adjustments _____

_____

Supplements _____

_____

Self-Care _____

_____

Best Thing That Happened Today _____

_____

Day of Cycle _____   Moon Phase_____

How I'm Feeling 1 2 3 4 5 6 7 8 9 10

_____

_____

_____

_____

_____

_____

_____

_____

_____

_____

_____

_____

_____

_____

_____

_____

_____

_____

_____

_____

_____

_____

Date _____

Medication _____ Adjustments _____

_____

Supplements _____

_____

Self-Care _____

_____

Best Thing That Happened Today _____

_____

Day of Cycle _____ Moon Phase _____

How I'm Feeling 1 2 3 4 5 6 7 8 9 10

_____

_____

_____

_____

_____

_____

_____

_____

_____

_____

_____

_____

_____

_____

_____

_____

_____

_____

_____

_____

_____

_____

Date _____

Medication _____   Adjustments _____

_____

Supplements _____

_____

Self-Care _____

_____

Best Thing That Happened Today _____

_____

Day of Cycle _____   Moon Phase_____

How I'm Feeling 1 2 3 4 5 6 7 8 9 10

_____

_____

_____

_____

_____

_____

_____

_____

_____

_____

_____

_____

_____

_____

_____

_____

_____

_____

_____

_____

_____

_____

Date _____

Medication _____   Adjustments _____

_____

Supplements _____

_____

Self-Care _____

_____

Best Thing That Happened Today _____

_____

Day of Cycle _____   Moon Phase _____

How I'm Feeling 1 2 3 4 5 6 7 8 9 10

_____
_____
_____
_____
_____
_____
_____
_____
_____
_____
_____
_____
_____
_____
_____
_____
_____
_____
_____
_____
_____
_____
_____
_____
_____

Date ———————————

Medication ———————————————————— Adjustments ———————
————————————————————

Supplements ————————————————————
————————————————————

Self-Care ————————————————————————————

Best Thing That Happened Today ————————————————————————

Day of Cycle ———————— Moon Phase ———————

How I'm Feeling 1 2 3 4 5 6 7 8 9 10

————————————————————————————————
————————————————————————————————
————————————————————————————————
————————————————————————————————
————————————————————————————————
————————————————————————————————
————————————————————————————————
————————————————————————————————
————————————————————————————————
————————————————————————————————
————————————————————————————————
————————————————————————————————
————————————————————————————————
————————————————————————————————
————————————————————————————————
————————————————————————————————
————————————————————————————————
————————————————————————————————
————————————————————————————————
————————————————————————————————
————————————————————————————————
————————————————————————————————
————————————————————————————————

Date _____

Medication _____   Adjustments _____

_____

Supplements _____

_____

Self-Care _____

_____

Best Thing That Happened Today _____

_____

Day of Cycle _____   Moon Phase _____

How I'm Feeling 1 2 3 4 5 6 7 8 9 10

_____

_____

_____

_____

_____

_____

_____

_____

_____

_____

_____

_____

_____

_____

_____

_____

_____

_____

_____

_____

_____

_____

_____

_____

_____

Date _____

Medication _____   Adjustments _____

_____

Supplements _____

_____

Self-Care _____

_____

Best Thing That Happened Today _____

_____

Day of Cycle _____   Moon Phase_____

How I'm Feeling 1 2 3 4 5 6 7 8 9 10

_____

_____

_____

_____

_____

_____

_____

_____

_____

_____

_____

_____

_____

_____

_____

_____

_____

_____

_____

_____

_____

_____

_____

Date _____

Medication _____   Adjustments _____

_____

Supplements _____

_____

Self-Care _____

_____

Best Thing That Happened Today _____

_____

Day of Cycle _____   Moon Phase _____

How I'm Feeling 1 2 3 4 5 6 7 8 9 10

_____

_____

_____

_____

_____

_____

_____

_____

_____

_____

_____

_____

_____

_____

_____

_____

_____

_____

_____

_____

_____

_____

_____

_____

Date _____

Medication _____   Adjustments _____

_____

Supplements _____

_____

Self-Care _____

_____

Best Thing That Happened Today _____

_____

Day of Cycle _____   Moon Phase _____

How I'm Feeling 1 2 3 4 5 6 7 8 9 10

_____
_____
_____
_____
_____
_____
_____
_____
_____
_____
_____
_____
_____
_____
_____
_____
_____
_____
_____
_____
_____
_____
_____
_____

Date _____

Medication _____   Adjustments _____

_____

Supplements _____

_____

Self-Care _____

_____

Best Thing That Happened Today _____

_____

Day of Cycle _____   Moon Phase _____

How I'm Feeling 1 2 3 4 5 6 7 8 9 10

_____

_____

_____

_____

_____

_____

_____

_____

_____

_____

_____

_____

_____

_____

_____

_____

_____

_____

_____

_____

_____

_____

_____

Date _____

Medication _____   Adjustments _____

_____

Supplements _____

_____

Self-Care _____

Best Thing That Happened Today _____

_____

Day of Cycle _____   Moon Phase _____

How I'm Feeling 1 2 3 4 5 6 7 8 9 10

_____

_____

_____

_____

_____

_____

_____

_____

_____

_____

_____

_____

_____

_____

_____

_____

_____

_____

_____

_____

_____

_____

_____

_____

_____

Date _____

Medication _____   Adjustments _____

_____

Supplements _____

_____

Self-Care _____

_____

Best Thing That Happened Today _____

_____

Day of Cycle _____   Moon Phase _____

How I'm Feeling 1 2 3 4 5 6 7 8 9 10

_____
_____
_____
_____
_____
_____
_____
_____
_____
_____
_____
_____
_____
_____
_____
_____
_____
_____
_____
_____
_____
_____
_____
_____

Date _____

Medication _____   Adjustments _____

_____

Supplements _____

_____

Self-Care _____

_____

Best Thing That Happened Today _____

_____

Day of Cycle _____   Moon Phase _____

How I'm Feeling 1 2 3 4 5 6 7 8 9 10

_____

_____

_____

_____

_____

_____

_____

_____

_____

_____

_____

_____

_____

_____

_____

_____

_____

_____

_____

_____

_____

_____

_____

Date _____

Medication _____ Adjustments _____
_____

Supplements _____
_____

Self-Care _____
_____

Best Thing That Happened Today _____
_____

Day of Cycle _____ Moon Phase _____

How I'm Feeling 1 2 3 4 5 6 7 8 9 10

_____
_____
_____
_____
_____
_____
_____
_____
_____
_____
_____
_____
_____
_____
_____
_____
_____
_____
_____
_____
_____
_____
_____
_____
_____
_____
_____

Date _____

Medication _____   Adjustments _____

_____

Supplements _____

_____

Self-Care _____

_____

Best Thing That Happened Today _____

_____

Day of Cycle _____   Moon Phase _____

How I'm Feeling 1 2 3 4 5 6 7 8 9 10

_____

_____

_____

_____

_____

_____

_____

_____

_____

_____

_____

_____

_____

_____

_____

_____

_____

_____

_____

_____

_____

_____

Date _____

Medication _____   Adjustments _____
_____

Supplements _____
_____

Self-Care _____
_____

Best Thing That Happened Today _____
_____

Day of Cycle _____   Moon Phase _____

How I'm Feeling 1 2 3 4 5 6 7 8 9 10

_____
_____
_____
_____
_____
_____
_____
_____
_____
_____
_____
_____
_____
_____
_____
_____
_____
_____
_____
_____
_____
_____
_____
_____
_____

Date _____

Medication _____ Adjustments _____

_____

Supplements _____

_____

Self-Care _____

_____

Best Thing That Happened Today _____

_____

Day of Cycle _____ Moon Phase _____

How I'm Feeling 1 2 3 4 5 6 7 8 9 10

_____

_____

_____

_____

_____

_____

_____

_____

_____

_____

_____

_____

_____

_____

_____

_____

_____

_____

_____

_____

_____

_____

_____

_____

_____

Date _____

Medication _____   Adjustments _____

_____

Supplements _____

_____

Self-Care _____

_____

Best Thing That Happened Today _____

_____

Day of Cycle _____   Moon Phase _____

How I'm Feeling 1 2 3 4 5 6 7 8 9 10

_____

_____

_____

_____

_____

_____

_____

_____

_____

_____

_____

_____

_____

_____

_____

_____

_____

_____

_____

_____

_____

Date _____

Medication _____   Adjustments _____

_____

Supplements _____

_____

Self-Care _____

_____

Best Thing That Happened Today _____

_____

Day of Cycle _____   Moon Phase_____

How I'm Feeling 1 2 3 4 5 6 7 8 9 10

_____

_____

_____

_____

_____

_____

_____

_____

_____

_____

_____

_____

_____

_____

_____

_____

_____

_____

_____

_____

_____

_____

Date _____

Medication _____   Adjustments _____

_____

Supplements _____

_____

Self-Care _____

_____

Best Thing That Happened Today _____

_____

Day of Cycle _____   Moon Phase _____

How I'm Feeling 1 2 3 4 5 6 7 8 9 10

_____
_____
_____
_____
_____
_____
_____
_____
_____
_____
_____
_____
_____
_____
_____
_____
_____
_____
_____
_____
_____
_____
_____
_____
_____
_____

Date ———————————

Medication ———————————————————— Adjustments ——————————

————————————————————————

Supplements ——————————————————

————————————————————————

Self-Care ———————————————————————————————

————————————————————————————————

Best Thing That Happened Today ————————————————————————

————————————————————————————————

Day of Cycle ————————— Moon Phase——————————

How I'm Feeling 1 2 3 4 5 6 7 8 9 10

———————————————————————————————

———————————————————————————————

———————————————————————————————

———————————————————————————————

———————————————————————————————

———————————————————————————————

———————————————————————————————

———————————————————————————————

———————————————————————————————

———————————————————————————————

———————————————————————————————

———————————————————————————————

———————————————————————————————

———————————————————————————————

———————————————————————————————

———————————————————————————————

———————————————————————————————

———————————————————————————————

———————————————————————————————

———————————————————————————————

———————————————————————————————

———————————————————————————————

———————————————————————————————

Date _____

Medication _____   Adjustments _____

_____

Supplements _____

_____

Self-Care _____

_____

Best Thing That Happened Today _____

_____

Day of Cycle _____   Moon Phase _____

How I'm Feeling 1 2 3 4 5 6 7 8 9 10

_____

_____

_____

_____

_____

_____

_____

_____

_____

_____

_____

_____

_____

_____

_____

_____

_____

_____

_____

_____

_____

_____

Date ———————————

Medication ——————————————————————   Adjustments ——————————
————————————————————————————

Supplements ——————————————————————
————————————————————————————

Self-Care ——————————————————————————————

Best Thing That Happened Today ——————————————————————————
——

Day of Cycle ——————   Moon Phase——————————

How I'm Feeling 1 2 3 4 5 6 7 8 9 10

———————————————————————————————————————
———————————————————————————————————————
———————————————————————————————————————
———————————————————————————————————————
———————————————————————————————————————
———————————————————————————————————————
———————————————————————————————————————
———————————————————————————————————————
———————————————————————————————————————
———————————————————————————————————————
———————————————————————————————————————
———————————————————————————————————————
———————————————————————————————————————
———————————————————————————————————————
———————————————————————————————————————
———————————————————————————————————————
———————————————————————————————————————
———————————————————————————————————————
———————————————————————————————————————
———————————————————————————————————————
———————————————————————————————————————
———————————————————————————————————————

Date _____

Medication _____   Adjustments _____

_____

Supplements _____

_____

Self-Care _____

_____

Best Thing That Happened Today _____

_____

Day of Cycle _____   Moon Phase _____

How I'm Feeling 1 2 3 4 5 6 7 8 9 10

_____

_____

_____

_____

_____

_____

_____

_____

_____

_____

_____

_____

_____

_____

_____

_____

_____

_____

_____

_____

_____

_____

_____

Date _____

Medication _____   Adjustments _____

_____

Supplements _____

_____

Self-Care _____

_____

Best Thing That Happened Today _____

_____

Day of Cycle _____   Moon Phase _____

How I'm Feeling 1 2 3 4 5 6 7 8 9 10

_____

_____

_____

_____

_____

_____

_____

_____

_____

_____

_____

_____

_____

_____

_____

_____

_____

_____

_____

_____

_____

_____

_____

_____

_____

Date _____

Medication_____   Adjustments _____

_____

Supplements _____

_____

Self-Care _____

_____

Best Thing That Happened Today _____

_____

Day of Cycle _____   Moon Phase_____

How I'm Feeling 1 2 3 4 5 6 7 8 9 10

_____

_____

_____

_____

_____

_____

_____

_____

_____

_____

_____

_____

_____

_____

_____

_____

_____

_____

_____

_____

_____

_____

_____

_____

Date _____

Medication _____   Adjustments _____

Supplements _____

Self-Care _____

Best Thing That Happened Today _____

Day of Cycle _____   Moon Phase_____

How I'm Feeling 1 2 3 4 5 6 7 8 9 10

_____

_____

_____

_____

_____

_____

_____

_____

_____

_____

_____

_____

_____

_____

_____

_____

_____

_____

_____

_____

_____

_____

Date _____

Medication _____   Adjustments _____

_____

Supplements _____

_____

Self-Care _____

_____

Best Thing That Happened Today _____

_____

Day of Cycle _____   Moon Phase _____

How I'm Feeling 1 2 3 4 5 6 7 8 9 10

_____

_____

_____

_____

_____

_____

_____

_____

_____

_____

_____

_____

_____

_____

_____

_____

_____

_____

_____

_____

_____

_____

_____

_____

_____

_____

Date _____

Medication _____   Adjustments _____

_____

Supplements _____

_____

Self-Care _____

_____

Best Thing That Happened Today _____

_____

Day of Cycle _____   Moon Phase_____

How I'm Feeling 1 2 3 4 5 6 7 8 9 10

_____

_____

_____

_____

_____

_____

_____

_____

_____

_____

_____

_____

_____

_____

_____

_____

_____

_____

_____

_____

_____

_____

_____

_____

_____

Date _____

Medication _____   Adjustments _____

_____

Supplements _____

_____

Self-Care _____

_____

Best Thing That Happened Today _____

_____

Day of Cycle _____   Moon Phase _____

How I'm Feeling 1 2 3 4 5 6 7 8 9 10

_____

_____

_____

_____

_____

_____

_____

_____

_____

_____

_____

_____

_____

_____

_____

_____

_____

_____

_____

_____

_____

_____

_____

_____

Date _____

Medication _____   Adjustments _____

_____

Supplements _____

_____

Self-Care _____

_____

Best Thing That Happened Today _____

_____

Day of Cycle _____   Moon Phase _____

How I'm Feeling 1 2 3 4 5 6 7 8 9 10

_____

_____

_____

_____

_____

_____

_____

_____

_____

_____

_____

_____

_____

_____

_____

_____

_____

_____

_____

_____

_____

_____

_____

_____

Date _____

Medication _____ Adjustments _____

_____

Supplements _____

_____

Self-Care _____

_____

Best Thing That Happened Today _____

_____

Day of Cycle _____   Moon Phase _____

How I'm Feeling 1 2 3 4 5 6 7 8 9 10

_____

_____

_____

_____

_____

_____

_____

_____

_____

_____

_____

_____

_____

_____

_____

_____

_____

_____

_____

_____

_____

_____

_____

_____

Date _____

Medication _____   Adjustments _____

_____

Supplements _____

_____

Self-Care _____

_____

Best Thing That Happened Today _____

_____

Day of Cycle _____   Moon Phase_____

How I'm Feeling 1 2 3 4 5 6 7 8 9 10

_____

_____

_____

_____

_____

_____

_____

_____

_____

_____

_____

_____

_____

_____

_____

_____

_____

_____

_____

_____

_____

_____

Date _____

Medication _____ Adjustments _____

_____

Supplements _____

_____

Self-Care _____

_____

Best Thing That Happened Today _____

_____

Day of Cycle _____ Moon Phase _____

How I'm Feeling 1 2 3 4 5 6 7 8 9 10

_____

_____

_____

_____

_____

_____

_____

_____

_____

_____

_____

_____

_____

_____

_____

_____

_____

_____

_____

_____

_____

_____

_____

_____

Date _____

Medication _____ Adjustments _____

_____

Supplements _____

_____

Self-Care _____

_____

Best Thing That Happened Today _____

_____

Day of Cycle _____ Moon Phase _____

How I'm Feeling 1 2 3 4 5 6 7 8 9 10

_____

_____

_____

_____

_____

_____

_____

_____

_____

_____

_____

_____

_____

_____

_____

_____

_____

_____

_____

_____

_____

_____

_____

_____

Date _____

Medication _____   Adjustments _____

_____

Supplements _____

_____

Self-Care _____

_____

Best Thing That Happened Today _____

_____

Day of Cycle _____   Moon Phase_____

How I'm Feeling 1 2 3 4 5 6 7 8 9 10

_____

_____

_____

_____

_____

_____

_____

_____

_____

_____

_____

_____

_____

_____

_____

_____

_____

_____

_____

_____

_____

_____

_____

_____

_____

_____

Date _____

Medication _____   Adjustments _____

_____

Supplements _____

_____

Self-Care _____

_____

Best Thing That Happened Today _____

_____

Day of Cycle _____   Moon Phase _____

How I'm Feeling 1 2 3 4 5 6 7 8 9 10

_____

_____

_____

_____

_____

_____

_____

_____

_____

_____

_____

_____

_____

_____

_____

_____

_____

_____

_____

_____

_____

_____

_____

_____

Date _____

Medication _____   Adjustments _____

_____

Supplements _____

_____

Self-Care _____

_____

Best Thing That Happened Today _____

_____

Day of Cycle _____   Moon Phase _____

How I'm Feeling 1 2 3 4 5 6 7 8 9 10

_____

_____

_____

_____

_____

_____

_____

_____

_____

_____

_____

_____

_____

_____

_____

_____

_____

_____

_____

_____

_____

_____

_____

_____

Date _____

Medication _____   Adjustments _____

_____

Supplements _____

_____

Self-Care _____

_____

Best Thing That Happened Today _____

_____

Day of Cycle _____   Moon Phase _____

How I'm Feeling 1 2 3 4 5 6 7 8 9 10

_____

_____

_____

_____

_____

_____

_____

_____

_____

_____

_____

_____

_____

_____

_____

_____

_____

_____

_____

_____

_____

_____

_____

_____

_____

Date _____

Medication_____   Adjustments _____

_____

Supplements _____

_____

Self-Care _____

_____

Best Thing That Happened Today _____

_____

Day of Cycle _____   Moon Phase_____

How I'm Feeling 1 2 3 4 5 6 7 8 9 10

_____

_____

_____

_____

_____

_____

_____

_____

_____

_____

_____

_____

_____

_____

_____

_____

_____

_____

_____

_____

_____

_____

_____

Date _____

Medication _____   Adjustments _____

_____

Supplements _____

_____

Self-Care _____

_____

Best Thing That Happened Today _____

_____

Day of Cycle _____   Moon Phase _____

How I'm Feeling 1 2 3 4 5 6 7 8 9 10

_____

_____

_____

_____

_____

_____

_____

_____

_____

_____

_____

_____

_____

_____

_____

_____

_____

_____

_____

_____

_____

_____

_____

Date _____

Medication _____   Adjustments _____

_____

Supplements _____

_____

Self-Care _____

_____

Best Thing That Happened Today _____

_____

Day of Cycle _____   Moon Phase _____

How I'm Feeling 1 2 3 4 5 6 7 8 9 10

_____

_____

_____

_____

_____

_____

_____

_____

_____

_____

_____

_____

_____

_____

_____

_____

_____

_____

_____

_____

_____

_____

_____

_____

_____

_____

Date _____

Medication _____   Adjustments _____

_____

Supplements _____

_____

Self-Care _____

_____

Best Thing That Happened Today _____

_____

Day of Cycle _____   Moon Phase _____

How I'm Feeling 1 2 3 4 5 6 7 8 9 10

_____

_____

_____

_____

_____

_____

_____

_____

_____

_____

_____

_____

_____

_____

_____

_____

_____

_____

_____

_____

_____

_____

_____

Date _____

Medication _____   Adjustments _____

_____

Supplements _____

_____

Self-Care _____

_____

Best Thing That Happened Today _____

_____

Day of Cycle _____   Moon Phase _____

How I'm Feeling 1 2 3 4 5 6 7 8 9 10

_____

_____

_____

_____

_____

_____

_____

_____

_____

_____

_____

_____

_____

_____

_____

_____

_____

_____

_____

_____

_____

_____

_____

_____

_____

Date _____

Medication _____   Adjustments _____
_____

Supplements _____

Self-Care _____

Best Thing That Happened Today _____

Day of Cycle _____   Moon Phase _____

How I'm Feeling 1 2 3 4 5 6 7 8 9 10

_____
_____
_____
_____
_____
_____
_____
_____
_____
_____
_____
_____
_____
_____
_____
_____
_____
_____
_____
_____
_____
_____
_____
_____

Date _____

Medication _____   Adjustments _____

_____

Supplements _____

_____

Self-Care _____

_____

Best Thing That Happened Today _____

_____

Day of Cycle _____   Moon Phase _____

How I'm Feeling 1 2 3 4 5 6 7 8 9 10

_____

_____

_____

_____

_____

_____

_____

_____

_____

_____

_____

_____

_____

_____

_____

_____

_____

_____

_____

_____

_____

_____

_____

Date _____

Medication _____   Adjustments _____

_____

Supplements _____

_____

Self-Care _____

_____

Best Thing That Happened Today _____

_____

Day of Cycle _____   Moon Phase _____

How I'm Feeling 1 2 3 4 5 6 7 8 9 10

_____

_____

_____

_____

_____

_____

_____

_____

_____

_____

_____

_____

_____

_____

_____

_____

_____

_____

_____

_____

_____

_____

_____

Date _____

Medication _____   Adjustments _____

_____

Supplements _____

_____

Self-Care _____

_____

Best Thing That Happened Today _____

_____

Day of Cycle _____   Moon Phase _____

How I'm Feeling 1 2 3 4 5 6 7 8 9 10

_____

_____

_____

_____

_____

_____

_____

_____

_____

_____

_____

_____

_____

_____

_____

_____

_____

_____

_____

_____

_____

_____

Date _____

Medication _____   Adjustments _____

_____

Supplements _____

_____

Self-Care _____

_____

Best Thing That Happened Today _____

_____

Day of Cycle _____   Moon Phase _____

How I'm Feeling 1 2 3 4 5 6 7 8 9 10

_____

_____

_____

_____

_____

_____

_____

_____

_____

_____

_____

_____

_____

_____

_____

_____

_____

_____

_____

_____

_____

_____

Date _____

Medication_____   Adjustments _____

_____

Supplements _____

_____

Self-Care _____

_____

Best Thing That Happened Today _____

_____

Day of Cycle _____   Moon Phase_____

How I'm Feeling 1 2 3 4 5 6 7 8 9 10

_____
_____
_____
_____
_____
_____
_____
_____
_____
_____
_____
_____
_____
_____
_____
_____
_____
_____
_____
_____
_____
_____
_____
_____

Date _____

Medication _____   Adjustments _____
_____

Supplements _____
_____

Self-Care _____
_____

Best Thing That Happened Today _____
_____

Day of Cycle _____   Moon Phase _____

How I'm Feeling 1 2 3 4 5 6 7 8 9 10

_____
_____
_____
_____
_____
_____
_____
_____
_____
_____
_____
_____
_____
_____
_____
_____
_____
_____
_____
_____
_____
_____
_____
_____
_____

Date _____

Medication _____   Adjustments _____

_____

Supplements _____

_____

Self-Care _____

_____

Best Thing That Happened Today _____

_____

Day of Cycle _____   Moon Phase _____

How I'm Feeling 1 2 3 4 5 6 7 8 9 10

_____

_____

_____

_____

_____

_____

_____

_____

_____

_____

_____

_____

_____

_____

_____

_____

_____

_____

_____

_____

_____

_____

_____

_____

_____

Date ————————————

Medication ———————————————————————   Adjustments ———————————

——————————————————————————

Supplements ———————————————————————

——————————————————————————

Self-Care ————————————————————————————————

————————————————————————————————

Best Thing That Happened Today ————————————————————————————

————————————————————————————————

Day of Cycle ———————   Moon Phase———————————

How I'm Feeling   1   2   3   4   5   6   7   8   9   10

—————————————————————————————————————

—————————————————————————————————————

—————————————————————————————————————

—————————————————————————————————————

—————————————————————————————————————

—————————————————————————————————————

—————————————————————————————————————

—————————————————————————————————————

—————————————————————————————————————

—————————————————————————————————————

—————————————————————————————————————

—————————————————————————————————————

—————————————————————————————————————

—————————————————————————————————————

—————————————————————————————————————

—————————————————————————————————————

—————————————————————————————————————

—————————————————————————————————————

—————————————————————————————————————

—————————————————————————————————————

—————————————————————————————————————

—————————————————————————————————————

—————————————————————————————————————

Date _____

Medication _____   Adjustments _____

_____

Supplements _____

_____

Self-Care _____

_____

Best Thing That Happened Today _____

_____

Day of Cycle _____   Moon Phase _____

How I'm Feeling 1 2 3 4 5 6 7 8 9 10

_____

_____

_____

_____

_____

_____

_____

_____

_____

_____

_____

_____

_____

_____

_____

_____

_____

_____

_____

_____

_____

_____

_____

_____

_____

_____

Date _____

Medication _____   Adjustments _____

_____

Supplements _____

_____

Self-Care _____

_____

Best Thing That Happened Today _____

_____

Day of Cycle _____   Moon Phase _____

How I'm Feeling 1 2 3 4 5 6 7 8 9 10

_____
_____
_____
_____
_____
_____
_____
_____
_____
_____
_____
_____
_____
_____
_____
_____
_____
_____
_____
_____
_____
_____
_____
_____
_____

Date _____

Medication _____ Adjustments _____

_____

Supplements _____

_____

Self-Care _____

_____

Best Thing That Happened Today _____

_____

Day of Cycle _____ Moon Phase _____

How I'm Feeling 1 2 3 4 5 6 7 8 9 10

_____

_____

_____

_____

_____

_____

_____

_____

_____

_____

_____

_____

_____

_____

_____

_____

_____

_____

_____

_____

_____

_____

_____

_____

Date _____

Medication _____ Adjustments _____

_____

Supplements _____

_____

Self-Care _____

_____

Best Thing That Happened Today _____

_____

Day of Cycle _____ Moon Phase _____

How I'm Feeling 1 2 3 4 5 6 7 8 9 10

_____

_____

_____

_____

_____

_____

_____

_____

_____

_____

_____

_____

_____

_____

_____

_____

_____

_____

_____

_____

_____

_____

_____

Date _____

Medication_____   Adjustments _____

_____

Supplements _____

_____

Self-Care _____

_____

Best Thing That Happened Today _____

_____

Day of Cycle _____   Moon Phase_____

How I'm Feeling 1 2 3 4 5 6 7 8 9 10

_____

_____

_____

_____

_____

_____

_____

_____

_____

_____

_____

_____

_____

_____

_____

_____

_____

_____

_____

_____

_____

_____

Date _____

Medication _____   Adjustments _____

_____

Supplements _____

_____

Self-Care _____

_____

Best Thing That Happened Today _____

_____

Day of Cycle _____   Moon Phase _____

How I'm Feeling 1 2 3 4 5 6 7 8 9 10

_____

_____

_____

_____

_____

_____

_____

_____

_____

_____

_____

_____

_____

_____

_____

_____

_____

_____

_____

_____

_____

_____

_____

_____

_____

Date _____

Medication _____   Adjustments _____

_____

Supplements _____

_____

Self-Care _____

_____

Best Thing That Happened Today _____

_____

Day of Cycle _____   Moon Phase _____

How I'm Feeling 1 2 3 4 5 6 7 8 9 10

_____

_____

_____

_____

_____

_____

_____

_____

_____

_____

_____

_____

_____

_____

_____

_____

_____

_____

_____

_____

_____

_____

_____

Date _____

Medication _____   Adjustments _____
_____

Supplements _____
_____

Self-Care _____
_____

Best Thing That Happened Today _____
_____

Day of Cycle _____   Moon Phase _____

How I'm Feeling 1 2 3 4 5 6 7 8 9 10

_____
_____
_____
_____
_____
_____
_____
_____
_____
_____
_____
_____
_____
_____
_____
_____
_____
_____
_____
_____
_____
_____
_____
_____

Date _____

Medication _____   Adjustments _____

_____

Supplements _____

_____

Self-Care _____

_____

Best Thing That Happened Today _____

_____

Day of Cycle _____   Moon Phase _____

How I'm Feeling 1 2 3 4 5 6 7 8 9 10

_____
_____
_____
_____
_____
_____
_____
_____
_____
_____
_____
_____
_____
_____
_____
_____
_____
_____
_____
_____
_____
_____
_____
_____

Date _____

Medication _____   Adjustments _____
_____

Supplements _____

Self-Care _____

Best Thing That Happened Today _____

Day of Cycle _____   Moon Phase _____

How I'm Feeling 1 2 3 4 5 6 7 8 9 10

_____

_____

_____

_____

_____

_____

_____

_____

_____

_____

_____

_____

_____

_____

_____

_____

_____

_____

_____

_____

_____

_____

Date _____

Medication_____   Adjustments _____

_____

Supplements _____

_____

Self-Care _____

_____

Best Thing That Happened Today _____

_____

Day of Cycle _____   Moon Phase_____

How I'm Feeling 1 2 3 4 5 6 7 8 9 10

_____

_____

_____

_____

_____

_____

_____

_____

_____

_____

_____

_____

_____

_____

_____

_____

_____

_____

_____

_____

_____

_____

_____

Date _____

Medication _____   Adjustments _____

_____

Supplements _____

_____

Self-Care _____

_____

Best Thing That Happened Today _____

_____

Day of Cycle _____   Moon Phase _____

How I'm Feeling 1 2 3 4 5 6 7 8 9 10

_____

_____

_____

_____

_____

_____

_____

_____

_____

_____

_____

_____

_____

_____

_____

_____

_____

_____

_____

_____

_____

_____

_____

Date _____

Medication _____   Adjustments _____

_____

Supplements _____

_____

Self-Care _____

_____

Best Thing That Happened Today _____

_____

Day of Cycle _____   Moon Phase _____

How I'm Feeling 1 2 3 4 5 6 7 8 9 10

_____

_____

_____

_____

_____

_____

_____

_____

_____

_____

_____

_____

_____

_____

_____

_____

_____

_____

_____

_____

_____

_____

_____

_____

Date _____

Medication _____   Adjustments _____

_____

Supplements _____

_____

Self-Care _____

_____

Best Thing That Happened Today _____

_____

Day of Cycle _____   Moon Phase _____

How I'm Feeling 1 2 3 4 5 6 7 8 9 10

_____

_____

_____

_____

_____

_____

_____

_____

_____

_____

_____

_____

_____

_____

_____

_____

_____

_____

_____

_____

_____

_____

_____

Date _____

Medication_____   Adjustments _____

_____

Supplements _____

_____

Self-Care _____

_____

Best Thing That Happened Today _____

_____

Day of Cycle _____   Moon Phase_____

How I'm Feeling 1 2 3 4 5 6 7 8 9 10

_____
_____
_____
_____
_____
_____
_____
_____
_____
_____
_____
_____
_____
_____
_____
_____
_____
_____
_____
_____
_____
_____
_____

Date _____

Medication _____   Adjustments _____

_____

Supplements _____

_____

Self-Care_____

_____

Best Thing That Happened Today _____

_____

Day of Cycle _____   Moon Phase_____

How I'm Feeling 1 2 3 4 5 6 7 8 9 10

_____

_____

_____

_____

_____

_____

_____

_____

_____

_____

_____

_____

_____

_____

_____

_____

_____

_____

_____

_____

_____

_____

_____

Date _____

Medication _____ Adjustments _____

_____

Supplements _____

_____

Self-Care _____

_____

Best Thing That Happened Today _____

_____

Day of Cycle _____ Moon Phase _____

How I'm Feeling 1 2 3 4 5 6 7 8 9 10

_____
_____
_____
_____
_____
_____
_____
_____
_____
_____
_____
_____
_____
_____
_____
_____
_____
_____
_____
_____
_____
_____
_____
_____
_____
_____

Date _____

Medication _____   Adjustments _____

_____

Supplements _____

_____

Self-Care _____

_____

Best Thing That Happened Today _____

_____

Day of Cycle _____   Moon Phase _____

How I'm Feeling 1 2 3 4 5 6 7 8 9 10

_____

_____

_____

_____

_____

_____

_____

_____

_____

_____

_____

_____

_____

_____

_____

_____

_____

_____

_____

_____

_____

_____

_____

_____

Date _____

Medication _____   Adjustments _____

_____

Supplements _____

_____

Self-Care _____

_____

Best Thing That Happened Today _____

_____

Day of Cycle _____   Moon Phase _____

How I'm Feeling 1 2 3 4 5 6 7 8 9 10

_____

_____

_____

_____

_____

_____

_____

_____

_____

_____

_____

_____

_____

_____

_____

_____

_____

_____

_____

_____

_____

_____

_____

_____

_____

Date _____

Medication _____ Adjustments _____

_____

Supplements _____

_____

Self-Care _____

_____

Best Thing That Happened Today _____

_____

Day of Cycle _____ Moon Phase _____

How I'm Feeling 1 2 3 4 5 6 7 8 9 10

_____
_____
_____
_____
_____
_____
_____
_____
_____
_____
_____
_____
_____
_____
_____
_____
_____
_____
_____
_____
_____
_____
_____
_____
_____

Date _____

Medication_____   Adjustments _____

_____

Supplements _____

_____

Self-Care _____

_____

Best Thing That Happened Today _____

_____

Day of Cycle _____   Moon Phase_____

How I'm Feeling 1 2 3 4 5 6 7 8 9 10

_____

_____

_____

_____

_____

_____

_____

_____

_____

_____

_____

_____

_____

_____

_____

_____

_____

_____

_____

_____

_____

_____

_____

_____

_____

Date _____

Medication _____   Adjustments _____

_____

Supplements _____

_____

Self-Care _____

_____

Best Thing That Happened Today _____

_____

Day of Cycle _____   Moon Phase_____

How I'm Feeling 1 2 3 4 5 6 7 8 9 10

_____

_____

_____

_____

_____

_____

_____

_____

_____

_____

_____

_____

_____

_____

_____

_____

_____

_____

_____

_____

_____

_____

Date _____

Medication _____   Adjustments _____

_____

Supplements _____

_____

Self-Care _____

_____

Best Thing That Happened Today _____

_____

Day of Cycle _____   Moon Phase _____

How I'm Feeling 1 2 3 4 5 6 7 8 9 10

_____

_____

_____

_____

_____

_____

_____

_____

_____

_____

_____

_____

_____

_____

_____

_____

_____

_____

_____

_____

_____

_____

_____

_____

Date _____

Medication _____   Adjustments _____

_____

Supplements _____

_____

Self-Care _____

_____

Best Thing That Happened Today _____

_____

Day of Cycle _____   Moon Phase _____

How I'm Feeling 1 2 3 4 5 6 7 8 9 10

_____

_____

_____

_____

_____

_____

_____

_____

_____

_____

_____

_____

_____

_____

_____

_____

_____

_____

_____

_____

_____

_____

_____

_____

_____

Date _____

Medication _____   Adjustments _____
_____

Supplements _____
_____

Self-Care _____
_____

Best Thing That Happened Today _____
_____

Day of Cycle _____   Moon Phase _____

How I'm Feeling 1 2 3 4 5 6 7 8 9 10

_____
_____
_____
_____
_____
_____
_____
_____
_____
_____
_____
_____
_____
_____
_____
_____
_____
_____
_____
_____
_____
_____
_____
_____

Date _____

Medication _____   Adjustments _____

_____

Supplements _____

_____

Self-Care _____

_____

Best Thing That Happened Today _____

_____

Day of Cycle _____   Moon Phase_____

How I'm Feeling 1 2 3 4 5 6 7 8 9 10

_____

_____

_____

_____

_____

_____

_____

_____

_____

_____

_____

_____

_____

_____

_____

_____

_____

_____

_____

_____

_____

_____

_____

_____

Date _____

Medication _____ Adjustments _____

_____

Supplements _____

_____

Self-Care _____

_____

Best Thing That Happened Today _____

_____

Day of Cycle _____ Moon Phase_____

How I'm Feeling 1 2 3 4 5 6 7 8 9 10

_____

_____

_____

_____

_____

_____

_____

_____

_____

_____

_____

_____

_____

_____

_____

_____

_____

_____

_____

_____

_____

_____

_____

_____

Date ————————————

Medication ————————————————————————   Adjustments ——————————

————————————————————————————————

Supplements ——————————————————————————

————————————————————————————————

Self-Care ————————————————————————————————————

——

Best Thing That Happened Today ————————————————————————————————

——

Day of Cycle ——————   Moon Phase——————————

How I'm Feeling 1 2 3 4 5 6 7 8 9 10

——
——
——
——
——
——
——
——
——
——
——
——
——
——
——
——
——
——
——
——
——
——
——
——

Date _____

Medication _____   Adjustments _____

_____

Supplements _____

_____

Self-Care _____

_____

Best Thing That Happened Today _____

_____

Day of Cycle _____   Moon Phase _____

How I'm Feeling 1 2 3 4 5 6 7 8 9 10

_____
_____
_____
_____
_____
_____
_____
_____
_____
_____
_____
_____
_____
_____
_____
_____
_____
_____
_____
_____
_____
_____
_____

Date _____

Medication _____   Adjustments _____
_____

Supplements _____
_____

Self-Care _____

Best Thing That Happened Today _____
_____

Day of Cycle _____   Moon Phase _____

How I'm Feeling 1 2 3 4 5 6 7 8 9 10

_____
_____
_____
_____
_____
_____
_____
_____
_____
_____
_____
_____
_____
_____
_____
_____
_____
_____
_____
_____
_____
_____
_____
_____
_____

Date _____

Medication _____   Adjustments _____

_____

Supplements _____

_____

Self-Care _____

_____

Best Thing That Happened Today _____

_____

Day of Cycle _____   Moon Phase _____

How I'm Feeling 1 2 3 4 5 6 7 8 9 10

_____
_____
_____
_____
_____
_____
_____
_____
_____
_____
_____
_____
_____
_____
_____
_____
_____
_____
_____
_____
_____
_____
_____
_____
_____
_____
_____

Date _____

Medication _____   Adjustments _____

_____

Supplements _____

_____

Self-Care _____

_____

Best Thing That Happened Today _____

_____

Day of Cycle _____   Moon Phase _____

How I'm Feeling 1 2 3 4 5 6 7 8 9 10

_____

_____

_____

_____

_____

_____

_____

_____

_____

_____

_____

_____

_____

_____

_____

_____

_____

_____

_____

_____

_____

_____

_____

_____

Date _____

Medication _____   Adjustments _____

_____

Supplements _____

_____

Self-Care _____

_____

Best Thing That Happened Today _____

_____

Day of Cycle _____   Moon Phase _____

How I'm Feeling 1 2 3 4 5 6 7 8 9 10

_____

_____

_____

_____

_____

_____

_____

_____

_____

_____

_____

_____

_____

_____

_____

_____

_____

_____

_____

_____

_____

_____

Date _____

Medication _____   Adjustments _____
_____

Supplements _____
_____

Self-Care _____

Best Thing That Happened Today _____
_____

Day of Cycle _____   Moon Phase_____

How I'm Feeling 1 2 3 4 5 6 7 8 9 10

_____
_____
_____
_____
_____
_____
_____
_____
_____
_____
_____
_____
_____
_____
_____
_____
_____
_____
_____
_____
_____
_____
_____
_____
_____

Date _____

Medication _____   Adjustments _____

_____

Supplements _____

_____

Self-Care _____

_____

Best Thing That Happened Today _____

_____

Day of Cycle _____   Moon Phase _____

How I'm Feeling 1 2 3 4 5 6 7 8 9 10

_____

_____

_____

_____

_____

_____

_____

_____

_____

_____

_____

_____

_____

_____

_____

_____

_____

_____

_____

_____

_____

_____

_____

_____

_____

_____

Date _____

Medication _____ Adjustments _____

_____

Supplements _____

_____

Self-Care _____

_____

Best Thing That Happened Today _____

_____

Day of Cycle _____ Moon Phase_____

How I'm Feeling 1 2 3 4 5 6 7 8 9 10

_____

_____

_____

_____

_____

_____

_____

_____

_____

_____

_____

_____

_____

_____

_____

_____

_____

_____

_____

_____

_____

_____

_____

_____

_____

Date _____

Medication _____   Adjustments _____

_____

Supplements _____

_____

Self-Care _____

_____

Best Thing That Happened Today _____

_____

Day of Cycle _____   Moon Phase _____

How I'm Feeling 1 2 3 4 5 6 7 8 9 10

_____

_____

_____

_____

_____

_____

_____

_____

_____

_____

_____

_____

_____

_____

_____

_____

_____

_____

_____

_____

_____

_____

_____

_____

_____

Date ——————————

Medication _____   Adjustments _____

_____

Supplements _____

_____

Self-Care _____

Best Thing That Happened Today _____

_____

Day of Cycle _____   Moon Phase_____

How I'm Feeling 1 2 3 4 5 6 7 8 9 10

_____

_____

_____

_____

_____

_____

_____

_____

_____

_____

_____

_____

_____

_____

_____

_____

_____

_____

_____

_____

_____

_____

_____

Date _____

Medication _____   Adjustments _____

_____

Supplements _____

_____

Self-Care _____

_____

Best Thing That Happened Today _____

_____

Day of Cycle _____   Moon Phase _____

How I'm Feeling 1 2 3 4 5 6 7 8 9 10

_____

_____

_____

_____

_____

_____

_____

_____

_____

_____

_____

_____

_____

_____

_____

_____

_____

_____

_____

_____

_____

_____

_____

_____

Date _____

Medication _____   Adjustments _____

_____

Supplements _____

_____

Self-Care _____

_____

Best Thing That Happened Today _____

_____

Day of Cycle _____   Moon Phase_____

How I'm Feeling 1 2 3 4 5 6 7 8 9 10

_____

_____

_____

_____

_____

_____

_____

_____

_____

_____

_____

_____

_____

_____

_____

_____

_____

_____

_____

_____

_____

_____

Date _____

Medication _____   Adjustments _____

_____

Supplements _____

_____

Self-Care _____

_____

Best Thing That Happened Today _____

_____

Day of Cycle _____   Moon Phase _____

How I'm Feeling 1 2 3 4 5 6 7 8 9 10

_____

_____

_____

_____

_____

_____

_____

_____

_____

_____

_____

_____

_____

_____

_____

_____

_____

_____

_____

_____

_____

_____

_____

_____

_____

_____

Date _____

Medication _____   Adjustments _____

_____

Supplements _____

_____

Self-Care _____

_____

Best Thing That Happened Today _____

_____

Day of Cycle _____   Moon Phase _____

How I'm Feeling   1   2   3   4   5   6   7   8   9   10

_____

_____

_____

_____

_____

_____

_____

_____

_____

_____

_____

_____

_____

_____

_____

_____

_____

_____

_____

_____

_____

_____

_____

Date _____

Medication _____   Adjustments _____

_____

Supplements _____

_____

Self-Care _____

_____

Best Thing That Happened Today _____

_____

Day of Cycle _____   Moon Phase _____

How I'm Feeling 1 2 3 4 5 6 7 8 9 10

_____

_____

_____

_____

_____

_____

_____

_____

_____

_____

_____

_____

_____

_____

_____

_____

_____

_____

_____

_____

_____

_____

_____

Date _____

Medication _____   Adjustments _____

_____

Supplements _____

_____

Self-Care _____

Best Thing That Happened Today _____

Day of Cycle _____   Moon Phase _____

How I'm Feeling 1 2 3 4 5 6 7 8 9 10

_____
_____
_____
_____
_____
_____
_____
_____
_____
_____
_____
_____
_____
_____
_____
_____
_____
_____
_____
_____
_____
_____
_____
_____

Date _____

Medication _____   Adjustments _____

_____

Supplements _____

_____

Self-Care _____

_____

Best Thing That Happened Today _____

_____

Day of Cycle _____   Moon Phase _____

How I'm Feeling 1 2 3 4 5 6 7 8 9 10

_____

_____

_____

_____

_____

_____

_____

_____

_____

_____

_____

_____

_____

_____

_____

_____

_____

_____

_____

_____

_____

_____

_____

_____

Date _____

Medication _____   Adjustments _____

_____

Supplements _____

_____

Self-Care _____

_____

Best Thing That Happened Today _____

_____

Day of Cycle _____   Moon Phase _____

How I'm Feeling 1 2 3 4 5 6 7 8 9 10

_____

_____

_____

_____

_____

_____

_____

_____

_____

_____

_____

_____

_____

_____

_____

_____

_____

_____

_____

_____

_____

_____

_____

Date _____

Medication _____   Adjustments _____

_____

Supplements _____

_____

Self-Care _____

_____

Best Thing That Happened Today _____

_____

Day of Cycle _____   Moon Phase_____

How I'm Feeling 1 2 3 4 5 6 7 8 9 10

_____

_____

_____

_____

_____

_____

_____

_____

_____

_____

_____

_____

_____

_____

_____

_____

_____

_____

_____

_____

_____

_____

_____

_____

Date _____

Medication _____ Adjustments _____

_____

Supplements _____

_____

Self-Care _____

_____

Best Thing That Happened Today _____

_____

Day of Cycle _____   Moon Phase _____

How I'm Feeling 1 2 3 4 5 6 7 8 9 10

_____

_____

_____

_____

_____

_____

_____

_____

_____

_____

_____

_____

_____

_____

_____

_____

_____

_____

_____

_____

_____

_____

_____

Date _____

Medication _____   Adjustments _____

_____

Supplements _____

_____

Self-Care _____

_____

Best Thing That Happened Today _____

_____

Day of Cycle _____   Moon Phase _____

How I'm Feeling 1 2 3 4 5 6 7 8 9 10

_____

_____

_____

_____

_____

_____

_____

_____

_____

_____

_____

_____

_____

_____

_____

_____

_____

_____

_____

_____

_____

_____

_____

Date _____

Medication _____   Adjustments _____

_____

Supplements _____

_____

Self-Care _____

_____

Best Thing That Happened Today _____

_____

Day of Cycle _____   Moon Phase _____

How I'm Feeling 1 2 3 4 5 6 7 8 9 10

_____

_____

_____

_____

_____

_____

_____

_____

_____

_____

_____

_____

_____

_____

_____

_____

_____

_____

_____

_____

_____

_____

_____

Date _____

Medication _____   Adjustments _____

Supplements _____

Self-Care _____

Best Thing That Happened Today _____

Day of Cycle _____   Moon Phase _____

How I'm Feeling 1 2 3 4 5 6 7 8 9 10

_____

_____

_____

_____

_____

_____

_____

_____

_____

_____

_____

_____

_____

_____

_____

_____

_____

_____

_____

_____

_____

_____

_____

_____

Date _____

Medication _____   Adjustments _____

_____

Supplements _____

_____

Self-Care _____

_____

Best Thing That Happened Today _____

_____

Day of Cycle _____   Moon Phase_____

How I'm Feeling 1 2 3 4 5 6 7 8 9 10

_____

_____

_____

_____

_____

_____

_____

_____

_____

_____

_____

_____

_____

_____

_____

_____

_____

_____

_____

_____

_____

_____

_____

Date _____

Medication _____   Adjustments _____

_____

Supplements _____

_____

Self-Care _____

_____

Best Thing That Happened Today _____

_____

Day of Cycle _____   Moon Phase _____

How I'm Feeling 1 2 3 4 5 6 7 8 9 10

_____

_____

_____

_____

_____

_____

_____

_____

_____

_____

_____

_____

_____

_____

_____

_____

_____

_____

_____

_____

_____

_____

_____

Date _____

Medication _____   Adjustments _____

_____

Supplements _____

_____

Self-Care _____

_____

Best Thing That Happened Today _____

_____

Day of Cycle _____   Moon Phase _____

How I'm Feeling   1 2 3 4 5 6 7 8 9 10

_____

_____

_____

_____

_____

_____

_____

_____

_____

_____

_____

_____

_____

_____

_____

_____

_____

_____

_____

_____

_____

_____

_____

_____

Date _____

Medication _____ Adjustments _____

_____

Supplements _____

_____

Self-Care _____

_____

Best Thing That Happened Today _____

_____

Day of Cycle _____ Moon Phase _____

How I'm Feeling 1 2 3 4 5 6 7 8 9 10

_____

_____

_____

_____

_____

_____

_____

_____

_____

_____

_____

_____

_____

_____

_____

_____

_____

_____

_____

_____

_____

_____

_____

_____

Date _____

Medication _____   Adjustments _____

_____

Supplements _____

_____

Self-Care _____

_____

Best Thing That Happened Today _____

_____

Day of Cycle _____   Moon Phase _____

How I'm Feeling 1 2 3 4 5 6 7 8 9 10

_____
_____
_____
_____
_____
_____
_____
_____
_____
_____
_____
_____
_____
_____
_____
_____
_____
_____
_____
_____
_____
_____
_____
_____
_____

Date _____

Medication _____ Adjustments _____

_____

Supplements _____

_____

Self-Care _____

_____

Best Thing That Happened Today _____

_____

Day of Cycle _____ Moon Phase _____

How I'm Feeling 1 2 3 4 5 6 7 8 9 10

_____

_____

_____

_____

_____

_____

_____

_____

_____

_____

_____

_____

_____

_____

_____

_____

_____

_____

_____

_____

_____

_____

_____

_____

_____

Date _____

Medication _____   Adjustments _____

_____

Supplements _____

_____

Self-Care _____

_____

Best Thing That Happened Today _____

_____

Day of Cycle _____   Moon Phase _____

How I'm Feeling 1 2 3 4 5 6 7 8 9 10

_____

_____

_____

_____

_____

_____

_____

_____

_____

_____

_____

_____

_____

_____

_____

_____

_____

_____

_____

_____

_____

_____

_____

Date _____

Medication _____   Adjustments _____

_____

Supplements _____

_____

Self-Care _____

_____

Best Thing That Happened Today _____

_____

Day of Cycle _____   Moon Phase _____

How I'm Feeling 1 2 3 4 5 6 7 8 9 10

_____

_____

_____

_____

_____

_____

_____

_____

_____

_____

_____

_____

_____

_____

_____

_____

_____

_____

_____

_____

_____

_____

_____

Date _____

Medication _____   Adjustments _____

_____

Supplements _____

_____

Self-Care _____

_____

Best Thing That Happened Today _____

_____

Day of Cycle _____   Moon Phase _____

How I'm Feeling   1   2   3   4   5   6   7   8   9   10

_____

_____

_____

_____

_____

_____

_____

_____

_____

_____

_____

_____

_____

_____

_____

_____

_____

_____

_____

_____

_____

_____

_____

Date _____

Medication _____   Adjustments _____

_____

Supplements _____

_____

Self-Care _____

_____

Best Thing That Happened Today _____

_____

Day of Cycle _____   Moon Phase _____

How I'm Feeling 1 2 3 4 5 6 7 8 9 10

_____

_____

_____

_____

_____

_____

_____

_____

_____

_____

_____

_____

_____

_____

_____

_____

_____

_____

_____

_____

_____

_____

_____

_____

Date _____

Medication _____ Adjustments _____

_____

Supplements _____

_____

Self-Care _____

_____

Best Thing That Happened Today _____

_____

Day of Cycle _____ Moon Phase _____

How I'm Feeling 1 2 3 4 5 6 7 8 9 10

_____

_____

_____

_____

_____

_____

_____

_____

_____

_____

_____

_____

_____

_____

_____

_____

_____

_____

_____

_____

_____

_____

_____

Date _____

Medication _____ Adjustments _____

_____

Supplements _____

_____

Self-Care _____

_____

Best Thing That Happened Today _____

_____

Day of Cycle _____ Moon Phase _____

How I'm Feeling   1 2 3 4 5 6 7 8 9 10

_____

_____

_____

_____

_____

_____

_____

_____

_____

_____

_____

_____

_____

_____

_____

_____

_____

_____

_____

_____

_____

_____

_____

Date _____

Medication _____   Adjustments _____

_____

Supplements _____

_____

Self-Care _____

_____

Best Thing That Happened Today _____

_____

Day of Cycle _____   Moon Phase_____

How I'm Feeling 1 2 3 4 5 6 7 8 9 10

_____

_____

_____

_____

_____

_____

_____

_____

_____

_____

_____

_____

_____

_____

_____

_____

_____

_____

_____

_____

_____

_____

_____

Date _____

Medication _____   Adjustments _____

_____

Supplements _____

_____

Self-Care _____

_____

Best Thing That Happened Today _____

_____

Day of Cycle _____   Moon Phase _____

How I'm Feeling 1 2 3 4 5 6 7 8 9 10

_____
_____
_____
_____
_____
_____
_____
_____
_____
_____
_____
_____
_____
_____
_____
_____
_____
_____
_____
_____
_____
_____
_____
_____
_____

Date _____

Medication _____   Adjustments _____

_____

Supplements _____

_____

Self-Care _____

_____

Best Thing That Happened Today _____

_____

Day of Cycle _____   Moon Phase _____

How I'm Feeling 1 2 3 4 5 6 7 8 9 10

_____

_____

_____

_____

_____

_____

_____

_____

_____

_____

_____

_____

_____

_____

_____

_____

_____

_____

_____

_____

_____

_____

_____

Date _____

Medication _____   Adjustments _____

_____

Supplements _____

_____

Self-Care _____

_____

Best Thing That Happened Today _____

_____

Day of Cycle _____   Moon Phase _____

How I'm Feeling 1 2 3 4 5 6 7 8 9 10

_____

_____

_____

_____

_____

_____

_____

_____

_____

_____

_____

_____

_____

_____

_____

_____

_____

_____

_____

_____

_____

_____

_____

_____

Date _____

Medication _____   Adjustments _____

Supplements _____

_____

Self-Care _____

_____

Best Thing That Happened Today _____

_____

Day of Cycle _____   Moon Phase _____

How I'm Feeling 1 2 3 4 5 6 7 8 9 10

_____

_____

_____

_____

_____

_____

_____

_____

_____

_____

_____

_____

_____

_____

_____

_____

_____

_____

_____

_____

_____

_____

_____

_____

Date _____

Medication _____   Adjustments _____

_____

Supplements _____

_____

Self-Care _____

_____

Best Thing That Happened Today _____

_____

Day of Cycle _____   Moon Phase _____

How I'm Feeling 1 2 3 4 5 6 7 8 9 10

_____

_____

_____

_____

_____

_____

_____

_____

_____

_____

_____

_____

_____

_____

_____

_____

_____

_____

_____

_____

_____

_____

_____

_____

Date _____

Medication _____   Adjustments _____

_____

Supplements _____

_____

Self-Care _____

_____

Best Thing That Happened Today _____

_____

Day of Cycle _____   Moon Phase_____

How I'm Feeling 1 2 3 4 5 6 7 8 9 10

_____

_____

_____

_____

_____

_____

_____

_____

_____

_____

_____

_____

_____

_____

_____

_____

_____

_____

_____

_____

_____

_____

_____

_____

Date _____

Medication _____   Adjustments _____

_____

Supplements _____

_____

Self-Care _____

_____

Best Thing That Happened Today _____

_____

Day of Cycle _____   Moon Phase _____

How I'm Feeling 1 2 3 4 5 6 7 8 9 10

_____

_____

_____

_____

_____

_____

_____

_____

_____

_____

_____

_____

_____

_____

_____

_____

_____

_____

_____

_____

_____

_____

_____

Date _____

Medication _____   Adjustments _____

_____

Supplements _____

_____

Self-Care _____

_____

Best Thing That Happened Today _____

_____

Day of Cycle _____   Moon Phase _____

How I'm Feeling 1 2 3 4 5 6 7 8 9 10

_____

_____

_____

_____

_____

_____

_____

_____

_____

_____

_____

_____

_____

_____

_____

_____

_____

_____

_____

_____

_____

_____

Date _____

Medication _____ Adjustments _____

_____

Supplements _____

_____

Self-Care _____

_____

Best Thing That Happened Today _____

_____

Day of Cycle _____ Moon Phase _____

How I'm Feeling 1 2 3 4 5 6 7 8 9 10

_____

_____

_____

_____

_____

_____

_____

_____

_____

_____

_____

_____

_____

_____

_____

_____

_____

_____

_____

_____

_____

_____

_____

_____

Date _____

Medication _____   Adjustments _____

_____

Supplements _____

_____

Self-Care _____

_____

Best Thing That Happened Today _____

_____

Day of Cycle _____   Moon Phase _____

How I'm Feeling 1 2 3 4 5 6 7 8 9 10

_____

_____

_____

_____

_____

_____

_____

_____

_____

_____

_____

_____

_____

_____

_____

_____

_____

_____

_____

_____

_____

_____

_____

_____

Date _____

Medication _____   Adjustments _____
_____

Supplements _____
_____

Self-Care _____
_____

Best Thing That Happened Today _____
_____

Day of Cycle _____   Moon Phase _____

How I'm Feeling 1 2 3 4 5 6 7 8 9 10

_____
_____
_____
_____
_____
_____
_____
_____
_____
_____
_____
_____
_____
_____
_____
_____
_____
_____
_____
_____
_____
_____
_____
_____

Date _____

Medication _____   Adjustments _____

_____

Supplements _____

_____

Self-Care _____

_____

Best Thing That Happened Today _____

_____

Day of Cycle _____   Moon Phase _____

How I'm Feeling 1 2 3 4 5 6 7 8 9 10

_____

_____

_____

_____

_____

_____

_____

_____

_____

_____

_____

_____

_____

_____

_____

_____

_____

_____

_____

_____

_____

_____

_____

Date _____

Medication _____   Adjustments _____

_____

Supplements _____

_____

Self-Care _____

_____

Best Thing That Happened Today _____

_____

Day of Cycle _____   Moon Phase _____

How I'm Feeling 1 2 3 4 5 6 7 8 9 10

_____

_____

_____

_____

_____

_____

_____

_____

_____

_____

_____

_____

_____

_____

_____

_____

_____

_____

_____

_____

_____

_____

_____

_____

_____

Date _____

Medication _____ Adjustments _____

_____

Supplements _____

_____

Self-Care _____

_____

Best Thing That Happened Today _____

_____

Day of Cycle _____ Moon Phase _____

How I'm Feeling 1 2 3 4 5 6 7 8 9 10

_____

_____

_____

_____

_____

_____

_____

_____

_____

_____

_____

_____

_____

_____

_____

_____

_____

_____

_____

_____

_____

_____

_____

_____

_____

Date _____

Medication _____ Adjustments _____

_____

Supplements _____

_____

Self-Care _____

_____

Best Thing That Happened Today _____

_____

Day of Cycle _____ Moon Phase _____

How I'm Feeling 1 2 3 4 5 6 7 8 9 10

_____

_____

_____

_____

_____

_____

_____

_____

_____

_____

_____

_____

_____

_____

_____

_____

_____

Date _____

Medication _____   Adjustments _____
_____

Supplements _____
_____

Self-Care _____
_____

Best Thing That Happened Today _____
_____

Day of Cycle _____   Moon Phase _____

How I'm Feeling 1 2 3 4 5 6 7 8 9 10

_____
_____
_____
_____
_____
_____
_____
_____
_____
_____
_____
_____
_____
_____
_____
_____
_____
_____
_____
_____
_____
_____
_____
_____
_____
_____
_____

Date _____

Medication _____   Adjustments _____

_____

Supplements _____

_____

Self-Care _____

_____

Best Thing That Happened Today _____

_____

Day of Cycle _____   Moon Phase _____

How I'm Feeling 1 2 3 4 5 6 7 8 9 10

_____

_____

_____

_____

_____

_____

_____

_____

_____

_____

_____

_____

_____

_____

_____

_____

_____

_____

_____

_____

_____

_____

_____

Date _____

Medication _____   Adjustments _____

_____

Supplements _____

_____

Self-Care _____

_____

Best Thing That Happened Today _____

_____

Day of Cycle _____   Moon Phase_____

How I'm Feeling 1 2 3 4 5 6 7 8 9 10

_____
_____
_____
_____
_____
_____
_____
_____
_____
_____
_____
_____
_____
_____
_____
_____
_____
_____
_____
_____
_____
_____
_____
_____

Date _____

Medication_____   Adjustments _____
_____

Supplements _____

_____

Self-Care _____
_____

Best Thing That Happened Today _____
_____

Day of Cycle _____   Moon Phase_____

How I'm Feeling 1 2 3 4 5 6 7 8 9 10

_____
_____
_____
_____
_____
_____
_____
_____
_____
_____
_____
_____
_____
_____
_____
_____
_____
_____
_____
_____
_____
_____
_____

Date _____

Medication _____   Adjustments _____

_____

Supplements _____

_____

Self-Care _____

_____

Best Thing That Happened Today _____

_____

Day of Cycle _____   Moon Phase _____

How I'm Feeling 1 2 3 4 5 6 7 8 9 10

_____
_____
_____
_____
_____
_____
_____
_____
_____
_____
_____
_____
_____
_____
_____
_____
_____
_____
_____
_____
_____
_____
_____

Date _____

Medication _____   Adjustments _____

_____

Supplements _____

_____

Self-Care _____

_____

Best Thing That Happened Today _____

_____

Day of Cycle _____   Moon Phase _____

How I'm Feeling 1 2 3 4 5 6 7 8 9 10

_____

_____

_____

_____

_____

_____

_____

_____

_____

_____

_____

_____

_____

_____

_____

_____

_____

_____

_____

_____

_____

_____

_____

Date ———————————

Medication _____   Adjustments _____

_____

Supplements _____

_____

Self-Care _____

_____

Best Thing That Happened Today _____

_____

Day of Cycle _____   Moon Phase _____

How I'm Feeling 1 2 3 4 5 6 7 8 9 10

_____

_____

_____

_____

_____

_____

_____

_____

_____

_____

_____

_____

_____

_____

_____

_____

_____

_____

_____

_____

_____

_____

_____

_____

Date _____

Medication _____ Adjustments _____

_____

Supplements _____

_____

Self-Care _____

_____

Best Thing That Happened Today _____

_____

Day of Cycle _____ Moon Phase _____

How I'm Feeling 1 2 3 4 5 6 7 8 9 10

_____

_____

_____

_____

_____

_____

_____

_____

_____

_____

_____

_____

_____

_____

_____

_____

_____

_____

_____

_____

_____

_____

_____

_____

_____

_____

_____

Date _____

Medication _____ Adjustments _____

_____

Supplements _____

_____

Self-Care _____

_____

Best Thing That Happened Today _____

_____

Day of Cycle _____ Moon Phase _____

How I'm Feeling 1 2 3 4 5 6 7 8 9 10

_____

_____

_____

_____

_____

_____

_____

_____

_____

_____

_____

_____

_____

_____

_____

_____

_____

_____

_____

_____

_____

_____

_____

_____

Date _____

Medication _____   Adjustments _____

_____

Supplements _____

_____

Self-Care _____

_____

Best Thing That Happened Today _____

_____

Day of Cycle _____   Moon Phase _____

How I'm Feeling 1 2 3 4 5 6 7 8 9 10

_____

_____

_____

_____

_____

_____

_____

_____

_____

_____

_____

_____

_____

_____

_____

_____

_____

_____

_____

_____

_____

_____

_____

_____

Date _____

Medication _____   Adjustments _____

_____

Supplements _____

_____

Self-Care _____

_____

Best Thing That Happened Today _____

_____

Day of Cycle _____   Moon Phase _____

How I'm Feeling 1 2 3 4 5 6 7 8 9 10

_____

_____

_____

_____

_____

_____

_____

_____

_____

_____

_____

_____

_____

_____

_____

_____

_____

_____

_____

_____

_____

_____

Date _____

Medication _____   Adjustments _____

_____

Supplements _____

_____

Self-Care _____

_____

Best Thing That Happened Today _____

_____

Day of Cycle _____   Moon Phase _____

How I'm Feeling 1 2 3 4 5 6 7 8 9 10

_____

_____

_____

_____

_____

_____

_____

_____

_____

_____

_____

_____

_____

_____

_____

_____

_____

_____

_____

_____

_____

_____

_____

Date _____

Medication _____   Adjustments _____

_____

Supplements _____

_____

Self-Care _____

_____

Best Thing That Happened Today _____

_____

Day of Cycle _____   Moon Phase _____

How I'm Feeling 1 2 3 4 5 6 7 8 9 10

_____
_____
_____
_____
_____
_____
_____
_____
_____
_____
_____
_____
_____
_____
_____
_____
_____
_____
_____
_____
_____
_____
_____
_____
_____

Date _____

Medication _____   Adjustments _____

_____

Supplements _____

_____

Self-Care _____

_____

Best Thing That Happened Today _____

_____

Day of Cycle _____   Moon Phase _____

How I'm Feeling 1 2 3 4 5 6 7 8 9 10

_____

_____

_____

_____

_____

_____

_____

_____

_____

_____

_____

_____

_____

_____

_____

_____

_____

_____

_____

_____

_____

_____

_____

_____

_____

Date _____

Medication _____   Adjustments _____

_____

Supplements _____

_____

Self-Care _____

_____

Best Thing That Happened Today _____

_____

Day of Cycle _____   Moon Phase_____

How I'm Feeling 1 2 3 4 5 6 7 8 9 10

_____

_____

_____

_____

_____

_____

_____

_____

_____

_____

_____

_____

_____

_____

_____

_____

_____

_____

_____

_____

_____

_____

_____

_____

Date _____

Medication _____   Adjustments _____

_____

Supplements _____

_____

Self-Care _____

_____

Best Thing That Happened Today _____

_____

Day of Cycle _____   Moon Phase _____

How I'm Feeling 1 2 3 4 5 6 7 8 9 10

_____

_____

_____

_____

_____

_____

_____

_____

_____

_____

_____

_____

_____

_____

_____

_____

_____

_____

_____

_____

_____

_____

_____

Date _____

Medication _____ Adjustments _____

_____

Supplements _____

_____

Self-Care _____

_____

Best Thing That Happened Today _____

_____

Day of Cycle _____ Moon Phase_____

How I'm Feeling 1 2 3 4 5 6 7 8 9 10

_____

_____

_____

_____

_____

_____

_____

_____

_____

_____

_____

_____

_____

_____

_____

_____

_____

_____

_____

_____

_____

_____

_____

_____

_____

Date _____

Medication _____   Adjustments _____
_____

Supplements _____
_____

Self-Care _____

Best Thing That Happened Today _____
_____

Day of Cycle _____   Moon Phase _____

How I'm Feeling 1 2 3 4 5 6 7 8 9 10

_____
_____
_____
_____
_____
_____
_____
_____
_____
_____
_____
_____
_____
_____
_____
_____
_____
_____
_____
_____
_____
_____
_____
_____
_____

Date ———————————

Medication _____   Adjustments _____

_____

Supplements _____

_____

Self-Care _____

_____

Best Thing That Happened Today _____

_____

Day of Cycle _____   Moon Phase _____

How I'm Feeling 1 2 3 4 5 6 7 8 9 10

_____
_____
_____
_____
_____
_____
_____
_____
_____
_____
_____
_____
_____
_____
_____
_____
_____
_____
_____
_____
_____
_____
_____
_____
_____

Date _____

Medication _____   Adjustments _____
_____

Supplements _____
_____

Self-Care _____
_____

Best Thing That Happened Today _____
_____

Day of Cycle _____   Moon Phase _____

How I'm Feeling 1 2 3 4 5 6 7 8 9 10

_____
_____
_____
_____
_____
_____
_____
_____
_____
_____
_____
_____
_____
_____
_____
_____
_____
_____
_____
_____
_____
_____
_____
_____

Date _____

Medication _____   Adjustments _____

_____

Supplements _____

_____

Self-Care _____

_____

Best Thing That Happened Today _____

_____

Day of Cycle _____   Moon Phase _____

How I'm Feeling 1 2 3 4 5 6 7 8 9 10

_____

_____

_____

_____

_____

_____

_____

_____

_____

_____

_____

_____

_____

_____

_____

_____

_____

_____

_____

_____

_____

_____

_____

_____

_____

Date _____

Medication _____   Adjustments _____

_____

Supplements _____

_____

Self-Care _____

_____

Best Thing That Happened Today _____

_____

Day of Cycle _____   Moon Phase _____

How I'm Feeling 1 2 3 4 5 6 7 8 9 10

_____

_____

_____

_____

_____

_____

_____

_____

_____

_____

_____

_____

_____

_____

_____

_____

_____

_____

_____

_____

_____

_____

_____

Date _____

Medication _____   Adjustments _____

_____

Supplements _____

_____

Self-Care _____

Best Thing That Happened Today _____

Day of Cycle _____   Moon Phase_____

How I'm Feeling 1 2 3 4 5 6 7 8 9 10

_____

_____

_____

_____

_____

_____

_____

_____

_____

_____

_____

_____

_____

_____

_____

_____

_____

_____

_____

_____

_____

_____

_____

Date _____

Medication _____   Adjustments _____

_____

Supplements _____

_____

Self-Care _____

_____

Best Thing That Happened Today _____

_____

Day of Cycle _____   Moon Phase _____

How I'm Feeling 1 2 3 4 5 6 7 8 9 10

_____

_____

_____

_____

_____

_____

_____

_____

_____

_____

_____

_____

_____

_____

_____

_____

_____

_____

_____

_____

_____

_____

_____

_____

Date _____

Medication _____   Adjustments _____

_____

Supplements _____

_____

Self-Care _____

_____

Best Thing That Happened Today _____

_____

Day of Cycle _____   Moon Phase _____

How I'm Feeling 1 2 3 4 5 6 7 8 9 10

_____

_____

_____

_____

_____

_____

_____

_____

_____

_____

_____

_____

_____

_____

_____

_____

_____

_____

_____

_____

_____

_____

_____

_____

Date _____

Medication_____   Adjustments _____

_____

Supplements _____

_____

Self-Care _____

_____

Best Thing That Happened Today _____

_____

Day of Cycle _____   Moon Phase_____

How I'm Feeling 1 2 3 4 5 6 7 8 9 10

_____

_____

_____

_____

_____

_____

_____

_____

_____

_____

_____

_____

_____

_____

_____

_____

_____

_____

_____

_____

_____

_____

_____

_____

_____

_____

Date _____

Medication _____ Adjustments _____

_____

Supplements _____

_____

Self-Care _____

_____

Best Thing That Happened Today _____

_____

Day of Cycle _____ Moon Phase _____

How I'm Feeling 1 2 3 4 5 6 7 8 9 10

_____

_____

_____

_____

_____

_____

_____

_____

_____

_____

_____

_____

_____

_____

_____

_____

_____

_____

_____

_____

_____

_____

_____

_____

Date _____

Medication _____   Adjustments _____

_____

Supplements _____

_____

Self-Care _____

_____

Best Thing That Happened Today _____

_____

Day of Cycle _____   Moon Phase _____

How I'm Feeling 1 2 3 4 5 6 7 8 9 10

_____

_____

_____

_____

_____

_____

_____

_____

_____

_____

_____

_____

_____

_____

_____

_____

_____

_____

_____

_____

_____

_____

_____

Date _____

Medication _____   Adjustments _____

_____

Supplements _____

_____

Self-Care _____

_____

Best Thing That Happened Today _____

_____

Day of Cycle _____   Moon Phase _____

How I'm Feeling 1 2 3 4 5 6 7 8 9 10

_____

_____

_____

_____

_____

_____

_____

_____

_____

_____

_____

_____

_____

_____

_____

_____

_____

_____

_____

_____

_____

_____

_____

_____

Date _____

Medication _____   Adjustments _____

_____

Supplements _____

_____

Self-Care _____

_____

Best Thing That Happened Today _____

_____

Day of Cycle _____   Moon Phase _____

How I'm Feeling 1 2 3 4 5 6 7 8 9 10

_____

_____

_____

_____

_____

_____

_____

_____

_____

_____

_____

_____

_____

_____

_____

_____

_____

_____

_____

_____

_____

_____

_____

Date _____

Medication _____ Adjustments _____

_____

Supplements _____

_____

Self-Care _____

_____

Best Thing That Happened Today _____

_____

Day of Cycle _____ Moon Phase _____

How I'm Feeling 1 2 3 4 5 6 7 8 9 10

_____

_____

_____

_____

_____

_____

_____

_____

_____

_____

_____

_____

_____

_____

_____

_____

_____

_____

_____

_____

_____

_____

_____

_____

Date _____

Medication_____   Adjustments _____

_____

Supplements _____

_____

Self-Care _____

_____

Best Thing That Happened Today _____

_____

Day of Cycle _____   Moon Phase_____

How I'm Feeling 1 2 3 4 5 6 7 8 9 10

_____

_____

_____

_____

_____

_____

_____

_____

_____

_____

_____

_____

_____

_____

_____

_____

_____

_____

_____

_____

_____

_____

_____

_____

_____

Date _____

Medication _____   Adjustments _____

_____

Supplements _____

_____

Self-Care _____

_____

Best Thing That Happened Today _____

_____

Day of Cycle _____   Moon Phase_____

How I'm Feeling 1 2 3 4 5 6 7 8 9 10

_____

_____

_____

_____

_____

_____

_____

_____

_____

_____

_____

_____

_____

_____

_____

_____

_____

_____

_____

_____

_____

_____

_____

_____

Date _____

Medication _____   Adjustments _____

_____

Supplements _____

_____

Self-Care _____

_____

Best Thing That Happened Today _____

_____

Day of Cycle _____   Moon Phase _____

How I'm Feeling 1 2 3 4 5 6 7 8 9 10

_____

_____

_____

_____

_____

_____

_____

_____

_____

_____

_____

_____

_____

_____

_____

_____

_____

_____

_____

_____

_____

_____

_____

Date _____

Medication _____   Adjustments _____

_____

Supplements _____

_____

Self-Care _____

_____

Best Thing That Happened Today _____

_____

Day of Cycle _____   Moon Phase _____

How I'm Feeling 1 2 3 4 5 6 7 8 9 10

_____

_____

_____

_____

_____

_____

_____

_____

_____

_____

_____

_____

_____

_____

_____

_____

_____

_____

_____

_____

_____

_____

_____

_____

Date _____

Medication _____   Adjustments _____

_____

Supplements _____

_____

Self-Care _____

_____

Best Thing That Happened Today _____

_____

Day of Cycle _____   Moon Phase _____

How I'm Feeling 1 2 3 4 5 6 7 8 9 10

_____

_____

_____

_____

_____

_____

_____

_____

_____

_____

_____

_____

_____

_____

_____

_____

_____

_____

_____

_____

_____

_____

_____

_____

Date _____

Medication _____   Adjustments _____
_____

Supplements _____
_____

Self-Care _____
_____

Best Thing That Happened Today _____
_____

Day of Cycle _____   Moon Phase _____

How I'm Feeling 1 2 3 4 5 6 7 8 9 10

_____
_____
_____
_____
_____
_____
_____
_____
_____
_____
_____
_____
_____
_____
_____
_____
_____
_____
_____
_____
_____
_____
_____
_____
_____

Date _____

Medication _____ Adjustments _____

_____

Supplements _____

_____

Self-Care _____

_____

Best Thing That Happened Today _____

_____

Day of Cycle _____ Moon Phase _____

How I'm Feeling 1 2 3 4 5 6 7 8 9 10

_____

_____

_____

_____

_____

_____

_____

_____

_____

_____

_____

_____

_____

_____

_____

_____

_____

_____

_____

_____

_____

_____

_____

Date _____

Medication _____   Adjustments _____

_____

Supplements _____

_____

Self-Care _____

_____

Best Thing That Happened Today _____

_____

Day of Cycle _____   Moon Phase _____

How I'm Feeling 1 2 3 4 5 6 7 8 9 10

_____

_____

_____

_____

_____

_____

_____

_____

_____

_____

_____

_____

_____

_____

_____

_____

_____

_____

_____

_____

_____

_____

_____

_____

_____

Date _____

Medication_____   Adjustments _____

_____

Supplements _____

_____

Self-Care _____

_____

Best Thing That Happened Today _____

_____

Day of Cycle _____   Moon Phase_____

How I'm Feeling 1 2 3 4 5 6 7 8 9 10

_____

_____

_____

_____

_____

_____

_____

_____

_____

_____

_____

_____

_____

_____

_____

_____

_____

_____

_____

_____

_____

_____

_____

_____

_____

Date _____

Medication _____   Adjustments _____

_____

Supplements _____

_____

Self-Care _____

_____

Best Thing That Happened Today _____

_____

Day of Cycle _____   Moon Phase _____

How I'm Feeling 1 2 3 4 5 6 7 8 9 10

_____

_____

_____

_____

_____

_____

_____

_____

_____

_____

_____

_____

_____

_____

_____

_____

_____

_____

_____

_____

_____

_____

_____

_____

_____

Date _____

Medication _____ Adjustments _____

_____

Supplements _____

_____

Self-Care _____

_____

Best Thing That Happened Today _____

_____

Day of Cycle _____   Moon Phase_____

How I'm Feeling 1 2 3 4 5 6 7 8 9 10

_____

_____

_____

_____

_____

_____

_____

_____

_____

_____

_____

_____

_____

_____

_____

_____

_____

_____

_____

_____

_____

_____

_____

_____

Date _____

Medication _____ Adjustments _____

_____

Supplements _____

_____

Self-Care _____

_____

Best Thing That Happened Today _____

_____

Day of Cycle _____ Moon Phase _____

How I'm Feeling 1 2 3 4 5 6 7 8 9 10

_____

_____

_____

_____

_____

_____

_____

_____

_____

_____

_____

_____

_____

_____

_____

_____

_____

_____

_____

_____

_____

_____

_____

_____

Date _____

Medication _____   Adjustments _____

_____

Supplements _____

_____

Self-Care _____

_____

Best Thing That Happened Today _____

_____

Day of Cycle _____   Moon Phase _____

How I'm Feeling 1 2 3 4 5 6 7 8 9 10

_____

_____

_____

_____

_____

_____

_____

_____

_____

_____

_____

_____

_____

_____

_____

_____

_____

_____

_____

_____

_____

_____

_____

_____

_____

Date _____

Medication _____   Adjustments _____

_____

Supplements _____

_____

Self-Care _____

_____

Best Thing That Happened Today _____

_____

Day of Cycle _____   Moon Phase _____

How I'm Feeling 1 2 3 4 5 6 7 8 9 10

_____

_____

_____

_____

_____

_____

_____

_____

_____

_____

_____

_____

_____

_____

_____

_____

_____

_____

_____

_____

_____

_____

_____

_____

_____

_____

Date _____

Medication _____   Adjustments _____

_____

Supplements _____

_____

Self-Care _____

_____

Best Thing That Happened Today _____

_____

Day of Cycle _____   Moon Phase _____

How I'm Feeling 1 2 3 4 5 6 7 8 9 10

_____

_____

_____

_____

_____

_____

_____

_____

_____

_____

_____

_____

_____

_____

_____

_____

_____

_____

_____

_____

_____

_____

_____

Date _____

Medication _____   Adjustments _____

_____

Supplements _____

_____

Self-Care _____

_____

Best Thing That Happened Today _____

_____

Day of Cycle _____   Moon Phase _____

How I'm Feeling 1 2 3 4 5 6 7 8 9 10

_____

_____

_____

_____

_____

_____

_____

_____

_____

_____

_____

_____

_____

_____

_____

_____

_____

_____

_____

_____

_____

_____

_____

Date _____

Medication _____ Adjustments _____

_____

Supplements _____

_____

Self-Care _____

Best Thing That Happened Today _____

Day of Cycle _____ Moon Phase _____

How I'm Feeling 1 2 3 4 5 6 7 8 9 10

_____

_____

_____

_____

_____

_____

_____

_____

_____

_____

_____

_____

_____

_____

_____

_____

_____

_____

_____

_____

_____

_____

_____

_____

Date _____

Medication _____   Adjustments _____

_____

Supplements _____

_____

Self-Care _____

_____

Best Thing That Happened Today _____

_____

Day of Cycle _____   Moon Phase _____

How I'm Feeling 1 2 3 4 5 6 7 8 9 10

_____

_____

_____

_____

_____

_____

_____

_____

_____

_____

_____

_____

_____

_____

_____

_____

_____

_____

_____

_____

_____

_____

_____

_____

_____

Date _____

Medication _____   Adjustments _____

_____

Supplements _____

_____

Self-Care _____

_____

Best Thing That Happened Today _____

_____

Day of Cycle _____   Moon Phase _____

How I'm Feeling 1 2 3 4 5 6 7 8 9 10

_____
_____
_____
_____
_____
_____
_____
_____
_____
_____
_____
_____
_____
_____
_____
_____
_____
_____
_____
_____
_____
_____
_____

Date _____

Medication _____   Adjustments _____

_____

Supplements _____

_____

Self-Care _____

_____

Best Thing That Happened Today _____

_____

Day of Cycle _____   Moon Phase _____

How I'm Feeling 1 2 3 4 5 6 7 8 9 10

_____

_____

_____

_____

_____

_____

_____

_____

_____

_____

_____

_____

_____

_____

_____

_____

_____

_____

_____

_____

_____

_____

_____

_____

Date _____

Medication _____   Adjustments _____

_____

Supplements _____

_____

Self-Care _____

_____

Best Thing That Happened Today _____

_____

Day of Cycle _____   Moon Phase _____

How I'm Feeling 1 2 3 4 5 6 7 8 9 10

_____

_____

_____

_____

_____

_____

_____

_____

_____

_____

_____

_____

_____

_____

_____

_____

_____

_____

_____

_____

_____

_____

_____

_____

Date _____

Medication _____   Adjustments _____

_____

Supplements _____

_____

Self-Care _____

_____

Best Thing That Happened Today _____

_____

Day of Cycle _____   Moon Phase _____

How I'm Feeling 1 2 3 4 5 6 7 8 9 10

_____

_____

_____

_____

_____

_____

_____

_____

_____

_____

_____

_____

_____

_____

_____

_____

_____

_____

_____

_____

_____

_____

_____

Date _____

Medication _____   Adjustments _____

_____

Supplements _____

_____

Self-Care _____

_____

Best Thing That Happened Today _____

_____

Day of Cycle _____   Moon Phase _____

How I'm Feeling 1 2 3 4 5 6 7 8 9 10

_____

_____

_____

_____

_____

_____

_____

_____

_____

_____

_____

_____

_____

_____

_____

_____

_____

_____

_____

_____

_____

_____

_____

Date ———————————

Medication _____   Adjustments _____

_____

Supplements _____

_____

Self-Care _____

_____

Best Thing That Happened Today _____

_____

Day of Cycle _____   Moon Phase _____

How I'm Feeling 1 2 3 4 5 6 7 8 9 10

_____

_____

_____

_____

_____

_____

_____

_____

_____

_____

_____

_____

_____

_____

_____

_____

_____

_____

_____

_____

_____

_____

_____

_____

Date _____

Medication _____   Adjustments _____

_____

Supplements _____

_____

Self-Care _____

_____

Best Thing That Happened Today _____

_____

Day of Cycle _____   Moon Phase _____

How I'm Feeling 1 2 3 4 5 6 7 8 9 10

_____

_____

_____

_____

_____

_____

_____

_____

_____

_____

_____

_____

_____

_____

_____

_____

_____

_____

_____

_____

_____

_____

_____

_____

_____

Date _____

Medication _____   Adjustments _____

_____

Supplements _____

_____

Self-Care _____

_____

Best Thing That Happened Today _____

_____

Day of Cycle _____   Moon Phase _____

How I'm Feeling 1 2 3 4 5 6 7 8 9 10

_____

_____

_____

_____

_____

_____

_____

_____

_____

_____

_____

_____

_____

_____

_____

_____

_____

_____

_____

_____

_____

_____

_____

Date _____

Medication _____   Adjustments _____
_____

Supplements _____

Self-Care _____
_____

Best Thing That Happened Today _____
_____

Day of Cycle _____   Moon Phase _____

How I'm Feeling 1 2 3 4 5 6 7 8 9 10

_____
_____
_____
_____
_____
_____
_____
_____
_____
_____
_____
_____
_____
_____
_____
_____
_____
_____
_____
_____
_____
_____
_____

Date _____

Medication _____   Adjustments _____

_____

Supplements _____

_____

Self-Care _____

_____

Best Thing That Happened Today _____

_____

Day of Cycle _____   Moon Phase _____

How I'm Feeling 1 2 3 4 5 6 7 8 9 10

_____

_____

_____

_____

_____

_____

_____

_____

_____

_____

_____

_____

_____

_____

_____

_____

_____

_____

_____

_____

_____

_____

_____

Date _____

Medication_____   Adjustments _____

_____

Supplements _____

_____

Self-Care _____

_____

Best Thing That Happened Today _____

_____

Day of Cycle _____   Moon Phase_____

How I'm Feeling 1 2 3 4 5 6 7 8 9 10

Date _____

Medication _____   Adjustments _____
_____

Supplements _____
_____

Self-Care _____
_____

Best Thing That Happened Today _____
_____

Day of Cycle _____   Moon Phase _____

How I'm Feeling 1 2 3 4 5 6 7 8 9 10

_____
_____
_____
_____
_____
_____
_____
_____
_____
_____
_____
_____
_____
_____
_____
_____
_____
_____
_____
_____
_____
_____
_____
_____
_____

Date _____

Medication _____   Adjustments _____

_____

Supplements _____

_____

Self-Care _____

_____

Best Thing That Happened Today _____

_____

Day of Cycle _____   Moon Phase _____

How I'm Feeling 1 2 3 4 5 6 7 8 9 10

_____

_____

_____

_____

_____

_____

_____

_____

_____

_____

_____

_____

_____

_____

_____

_____

_____

_____

_____

_____

_____

_____

_____

_____

Date _____

Medication _____   Adjustments _____
_____

Supplements _____
_____

Self-Care _____

Best Thing That Happened Today _____

Day of Cycle _____   Moon Phase _____

How I'm Feeling 1 2 3 4 5 6 7 8 9 10

_____
_____
_____
_____
_____
_____
_____
_____
_____
_____
_____
_____
_____
_____
_____
_____
_____
_____
_____
_____
_____
_____
_____
_____
_____
_____

Date _____

Medication _____   Adjustments _____

_____

Supplements _____

_____

Self-Care _____

_____

Best Thing That Happened Today _____

_____

Day of Cycle _____   Moon Phase _____

How I'm Feeling 1 2 3 4 5 6 7 8 9 10

_____

_____

_____

_____

_____

_____

_____

_____

_____

_____

_____

_____

_____

_____

_____

_____

_____

_____

_____

_____

_____

_____

_____

_____

Date _____

Medication _____   Adjustments _____

_____

Supplements _____

_____

Self-Care _____

_____

Best Thing That Happened Today _____

_____

Day of Cycle _____   Moon Phase _____

How I'm Feeling 1 2 3 4 5 6 7 8 9 10

_____

_____

_____

_____

_____

_____

_____

_____

_____

_____

_____

_____

_____

_____

_____

_____

_____

_____

_____

_____

_____

_____

_____

_____

_____

_____

Date _____

Medication _____ Adjustments _____
_____

Supplements _____
_____

Self-Care _____
_____

Best Thing That Happened Today _____
_____

Day of Cycle _____ Moon Phase _____

How I'm Feeling 1 2 3 4 5 6 7 8 9 10

_____
_____
_____
_____
_____
_____
_____
_____
_____
_____
_____
_____
_____
_____
_____
_____
_____
_____
_____
_____
_____
_____
_____
_____

Date _____

Medication _____   Adjustments _____

_____

Supplements _____

_____

Self-Care _____

Best Thing That Happened Today _____

_____

Day of Cycle _____   Moon Phase _____

How I'm Feeling 1 2 3 4 5 6 7 8 9 10

_____

_____

_____

_____

_____

_____

_____

_____

_____

_____

_____

_____

_____

_____

_____

_____

_____

_____

_____

_____

_____

_____

_____

_____

Date _____

Medication_____   Adjustments _____

_____

Supplements _____

_____

Self-Care _____

_____

Best Thing That Happened Today _____

_____

Day of Cycle _____   Moon Phase_____

How I'm Feeling 1 2 3 4 5 6 7 8 9 10

_____

_____

_____

_____

_____

_____

_____

_____

_____

_____

_____

_____

_____

_____

_____

_____

_____

_____

_____

_____

_____

_____

_____

_____

Date _____

Medication _____   Adjustments _____

_____

Supplements _____

_____

Self-Care _____

_____

Best Thing That Happened Today _____

_____

Day of Cycle _____   Moon Phase _____

How I'm Feeling 1 2 3 4 5 6 7 8 9 10

_____

_____

_____

_____

_____

_____

_____

_____

_____

_____

_____

_____

_____

_____

_____

_____

_____

_____

_____

_____

_____

_____

_____

_____

_____

Date _____

Medication _____   Adjustments _____

_____

Supplements _____

_____

Self-Care _____

_____

Best Thing That Happened Today _____

_____

Day of Cycle _____   Moon Phase_____

How I'm Feeling 1 2 3 4 5 6 7 8 9 10

_____

_____

_____

_____

_____

_____

_____

_____

_____

_____

_____

_____

_____

_____

_____

_____

_____

_____

_____

_____

_____

_____

_____

_____

_____

Date _____

Medication _____   Adjustments _____

_____

Supplements _____

_____

Self-Care _____

_____

Best Thing That Happened Today _____

_____

Day of Cycle _____   Moon Phase _____

How I'm Feeling 1 2 3 4 5 6 7 8 9 10

_____

_____

_____

_____

_____

_____

_____

_____

_____

_____

_____

_____

_____

_____

_____

_____

_____

_____

_____

_____

_____

_____

_____

Date _____

Medication _____   Adjustments _____

_____

Supplements _____

_____

Self-Care _____

_____

Best Thing That Happened Today _____

_____

Day of Cycle _____   Moon Phase _____

How I'm Feeling 1 2 3 4 5 6 7 8 9 10

_____

_____

_____

_____

_____

_____

_____

_____

_____

_____

_____

_____

_____

_____

_____

_____

_____

_____

_____

_____

_____

_____

_____

_____

_____

Date _____

Medication _____ Adjustments _____

_____

Supplements _____

_____

Self-Care _____

_____

Best Thing That Happened Today _____

_____

Day of Cycle _____ Moon Phase _____

How I'm Feeling 1 2 3 4 5 6 7 8 9 10

_____

_____

_____

_____

_____

_____

_____

_____

_____

_____

_____

_____

_____

_____

_____

_____

_____

_____

_____

_____

_____

_____

_____

_____

_____

_____

Date _____

Medication _____   Adjustments _____

_____

Supplements _____

_____

Self-Care _____

_____

Best Thing That Happened Today _____

_____

Day of Cycle _____   Moon Phase _____

How I'm Feeling 1 2 3 4 5 6 7 8 9 10

_____

_____

_____

_____

_____

_____

_____

_____

_____

_____

_____

_____

_____

_____

_____

_____

_____

_____

_____

_____

_____

_____

_____

Date _____

Medication _____   Adjustments _____

_____

Supplements _____

_____

Self-Care _____

_____

Best Thing That Happened Today _____

_____

Day of Cycle _____   Moon Phase_____

How I'm Feeling 1 2 3 4 5 6 7 8 9 10

_____

_____

_____

_____

_____

_____

_____

_____

_____

_____

_____

_____

_____

_____

_____

_____

_____

_____

_____

_____

_____

_____

_____

_____

Date _____

Medication _____   Adjustments _____

_____

Supplements _____

_____

Self-Care _____

_____

Best Thing That Happened Today _____

_____

Day of Cycle _____   Moon Phase _____

How I'm Feeling 1 2 3 4 5 6 7 8 9 10

_____

_____

_____

_____

_____

_____

_____

_____

_____

_____

_____

_____

_____

_____

_____

_____

_____

_____

_____

_____

_____

_____

_____

_____

_____

_____

_____

Date _____

Medication _____   Adjustments _____
_____

Supplements _____
_____

Self-Care _____

Best Thing That Happened Today _____
_____

Day of Cycle _____   Moon Phase _____

How I'm Feeling 1 2 3 4 5 6 7 8 9 10

_____
_____
_____
_____
_____
_____
_____
_____
_____
_____
_____
_____
_____
_____
_____
_____
_____
_____
_____
_____
_____
_____
_____
_____
_____

Date _____

Medication _____   Adjustments _____

_____

Supplements _____

_____

Self-Care _____

_____

Best Thing That Happened Today _____

_____

Day of Cycle _____   Moon Phase _____

How I'm Feeling 1 2 3 4 5 6 7 8 9 10

_____

_____

_____

_____

_____

_____

_____

_____

_____

_____

_____

_____

_____

_____

_____

_____

_____

_____

_____

_____

_____

_____

_____

_____

_____

Date _____

Medication _____   Adjustments _____

_____

Supplements _____

_____

Self-Care _____

_____

Best Thing That Happened Today _____

_____

Day of Cycle _____   Moon Phase _____

How I'm Feeling 1 2 3 4 5 6 7 8 9 10

_____

_____

_____

_____

_____

_____

_____

_____

_____

_____

_____

_____

_____

_____

_____

_____

_____

_____

_____

_____

_____

_____

_____

_____

_____

_____

Date _____

Medication_____   Adjustments _____

_____

Supplements _____

_____

Self-Care _____

_____

Best Thing That Happened Today _____

_____

Day of Cycle _____   Moon Phase_____

How I'm Feeling 1 2 3 4 5 6 7 8 9 10

_____

_____

_____

_____

_____

_____

_____

_____

_____

_____

_____

_____

_____

_____

_____

_____

_____

_____

_____

_____

_____

_____

Date _____

Medication _____   Adjustments _____

_____

Supplements _____

_____

Self-Care _____

_____

Best Thing That Happened Today _____

_____

Day of Cycle _____   Moon Phase _____

How I'm Feeling 1 2 3 4 5 6 7 8 9 10

_____

_____

_____

_____

_____

_____

_____

_____

_____

_____

_____

_____

_____

_____

_____

_____

_____

_____

_____

_____

_____

_____

_____

_____

_____

_____

Date _____

Medication _____ Adjustments _____

_____

Supplements _____

_____

Self-Care _____

_____

Best Thing That Happened Today _____

_____

Day of Cycle _____ Moon Phase _____

How I'm Feeling 1 2 3 4 5 6 7 8 9 10

_____

_____

_____

_____

_____

_____

_____

_____

_____

_____

_____

_____

_____

_____

_____

_____

_____

_____

_____

_____

_____

_____

_____

_____

_____

Date _____

Medication _____   Adjustments _____

_____

Supplements _____

_____

Self-Care _____

_____

Best Thing That Happened Today _____

_____

Day of Cycle _____   Moon Phase _____

How I'm Feeling 1 2 3 4 5 6 7 8 9 10

_____

_____

_____

_____

_____

_____

_____

_____

_____

_____

_____

_____

_____

_____

_____

_____

_____

_____

_____

_____

_____

_____

_____

_____

_____

_____

Made in United States
Orlando, FL
07 July 2022

19528089R00212